T0313153

Portfolio
Management

Every owner of a physical copy of

Portfolio Management

can download the eBook for free in a DRM-free format that can be read on any eReader, tablet or smartphone.

Simply head to:

ebooks.harriman-house.com/portfoliomanagement

to get your copy now.

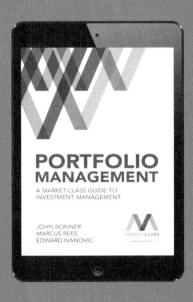

Portfolio
Management

A Market-Class Guide to Investment Management

John Bonner, Marcus Rees
& Edward Ivanovic

First edition published in 2014. This second edition published in 2015.

Copyright © JME Education (UK) Limited 2015

The right of John Bonner and Marcus Rees to be identified as the Authors has been asserted in accordance with the Copyright, Designs and Patents Act 1988.

Paperback ISBN: 978-0-85719-480-0
eBook ISBN: 978-0-85719-483-1

British Library Cataloguing in Publication Data
A CIP catalogue record for this book can be obtained from the British Library.

All rights reserved; no part of this publication may be reproduced, stored in a retrieval system, or transmitted in any form or by any means, electronic, mechanical, photocopying, recording, or otherwise without the prior written permission of the Publisher. This book may not be lent, resold, hired out or otherwise disposed of by way of trade in any form of binding or cover other than that in which it is published, without the prior written consent of the Publisher.

No responsibility for loss occasioned to any person or corporate body acting or refraining to act as a result of reading material in this book can be accepted by the Publisher or the Authors or the Employer of the Authors.

CONTENTS

ABOUT THE AUTHORS

JOHN BONNER – CHIEF EXECUTIVE OFFICER, JME EDUCATION (UK) LIMITED

John is the chief executive officer of JME Education (UK) Limited and the co-founder of the award-winning investment management simulator Market-Class (www.market-class.com).

John has an extensive background in developing products and services for the asset management and investment banking markets.

John's career includes co-founding a company that designed analysis and valuation tools for investment management and corporate finance professionals – a collaborative venture funded by Reuters and Goldman Sachs. John also worked for four years in corporate finance in the US, with responsibilities focused on company valuations, mergers and acquisitions, public equity offerings and private equity placements. He also managed Thomson Reuters' data operations centre in Europe, the operational hub for the management and support of all financial data in the region, as well as managing the portfolio of Finance & Risk, Legal and IP & Science content assets for Thomson Reuters.

John holds a patent for private company valuations and a patent pending for predictive initial public offering (IPO) analytics.

John completed his MBA at the University of Chicago and graduated cum laude (with honours) from the University of Minnesota with degrees in Economics, Finance and Actuarial Science.

MARCUS REES – CHIEF OPERATING OFFICER, JME EDUCATION (UK) LIMITED

Marcus is the chief operating officer of JME Education (UK) Limited and the co-founder of the award-winning investment management simulator Market-Class (www.market-class.com).

Marcus has 20 years' experience in the financial data services sector. His career has incorporated all aspects of data management: the sourcing and maintenance of real-time, contributed and proprietary financial data; data quality best practice process and improvement, including Six Sigma; customer experience design and continuous service improvement to meet the needs of the investment management community. He has extensive experience in internal communications and marketing communication roles. Marcus has also developed e-learning modules and produced peer-to-peer learning materials.

Marcus' role with JME Education (UK) Limited covers all aspects of sales, marketing and support, where he has grown the business globally. Market-Class achieved industry recognition in the 'Best Learning Game, Simulation or Virtual Environment' category at the 2010 E-Learning Awards.

Marcus graduated with honours from Oxford Brookes University with a BA in Economics and Politics, and he also holds a masters degree in Professional Management and Development from the University of Exeter.

EDWARD IVANOVIC – CHIEF TECHNOLOGY OFFICER, JME EDUCATION (UK) LIMITED

Edward is the chief technology officer of JME Education (UK) Limited and co-founder of the award-winning investment management simulator Market-Class (www.market-class.com).

Edward has over 20 years' experience in information technology and has worked primarily in the financial services industry. His experience spans co-founding start-up companies, designing algorithmic trading systems for Wall Street global investment banks, exchange simulators for the New York Stock Exchange, middle- and back-office systems for broker-dealers, trade compliance systems, and more.

Edward obtained a master's degree in Computer Science and Software Engineering from Melbourne University, Australia, with research in Natural Language Processing.

PORTFOLIO MANAGEMENT

1

Tell me and I'll forget; show me and I may remember; involve me and I'll understand.

Chinese proverb

CHAPTER 1.
WELCOME

INTRODUCTION

On the surface, investing can seem simple. The goal is to invest money so that over time you end up with more than you started out with.

While this may be the overall goal, there are an infinite number of ways to get there and an infinite number of ways to fail.

A smart investor doesn't rely on luck or 'guts', but instead focuses on learning as much as possible to make the best decisions. When you do this, you're more likely to reach your investment goals and control how you do so. For example, you may want to protect your money and avoid risk, or you may want to try to grow your money very quickly, no matter what the risk.

Investing is a highly complex pursuit. There is a myriad of elements to consider: political systems, political changes, social changes, industry and company fluctuations, as well as speculations. To sharpen your investment skills, there is no substitute for learning and practising (and reading as much as you can). **A Market-Class simulation is a great way to get started.**

Consider a scientist conducting research – she must learn as much as she can about all aspects of the experiment and then apply techniques over and over. Ultimately, the scientist learns the most by actually doing the research and testing her hypotheses.

Investing is no different: success requires both knowledge and experience. Participating in a Market-Class simulation provides both, and you're more likely to make smarter investment decisions when it comes to the real thing.

MARKET-CLASS: BOOK AND SIMULATION

This book has been designed and written as both a stand-alone text and as a complement to Market-Class, an online investment simulation where fund managers manage a $100m fund in a dynamic market and their decisions and those of their fellow fund managers 'make the market'. The intent of the book is to guide the reader through the key aspects of the fund management profession, working from a macro-industry overview to the micro details of security valuation techniques.

The value of this book is that it combines the benefits of academic experience with decades of industry experience – something also found in the complementary online Market-Class investment simulator. The book is written to be a valuable resource in its own right, as well as benefiting those using the book in conjunction with the simulator.

The result is a book that is both rich in content and reflective of the real-life workflow of portfolio management.

HOW THIS BOOK IS ORGANISED

This book starts with an introduction to the fund management industry before progressing through the details of asset valuation techniques and portfolio rebalancing.

The book is organised into the following parts, with each part ordered into chapters that dissect the content in more detail.

- Part 1 introduces the fund management sector, describing and explaining the size, relevance and importance of fund management and describing the key roles and functions performed within it.

- Part 2 goes into the next level of detail, describing the different types of fund that exist and how they differ from each other, before introducing the notion of the investible universe: the range of asset types that are typically available for investment purposes.

- Part 3 introduces the start of the workflow of the portfolio manager, explaining the concepts of investment objective setting and the importance of risk and return. It also covers the different types of risk that a portfolio manager must consider, before outlining the different investment strategies and philosophies that a portfolio manager might adopt.

- Part 4 focuses on the design, build and management of a portfolio: the practical aspects of a portfolio manager's workflow, how they allocate their funds, and the key techniques that are used in different asset classes to identify what to invest in, and the environment in which those decisions are made. The part closes by covering the importance and relevance of monitoring and rebalancing, the process by which a portfolio manager ensures that the ongoing performance of his portfolio or fund is aligned to his goals and objectives, with adjustments made accordingly.

- Part 5 focuses on the topics covered in the previous four parts in the context of a Market-Class simulation.

Interspersed throughout the book are examples using the characters of Bob, Samantha and Leo. These scenarios draw out the themes of portfolio management, presenting some of the challenges involved in making investment decisions in different roles.

A glossary of terms and a bibliography conclude the book.

We hope you enjoy the book and the simulation and learn from both. We encourage you to read and absorb information from all sources to help you make the most informed investment decisions possible.

John Bonner

Marcus Rees

CHAPTER 2.
PORTFOLIO MANAGEMENT

OBJECTIVES

1. **Introduce the subject of portfolio management.**

2. **Explain the key characteristics of the fund management industry.**

ASSET PORTFOLIO

Definition: An asset portfolio is a group of assets, such as cash, real estate, retirement funds, equities, fixed income and commodities, that are owned by an individual, company or government. Each asset in the portfolio often has different traits, most importantly anticipated return and expected risk.

Often an individual manages many of his or her own assets. With the purchase of funds or through an employer's pension scheme, a professional investment manager may manage some assets. An individual may work with a wealth manager in the management of his or her complete asset portfolio.

Importance: Understanding the scope of your asset portfolio is vital to properly manage your investments and ensure they reach your personal goals.

Example: The following is an individual's asset portfolio, showing which assets are managed by an investment manager.

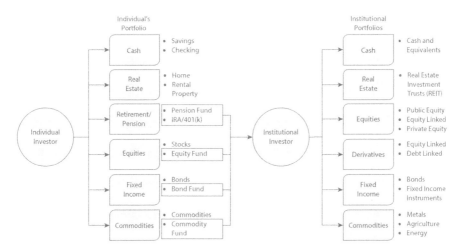

DELEGATED INVESTMENT MANAGEMENT

Definition: Delegated investment management means entrusting another person or firm to manage all or part of an investment portfolio.

The relationship between a portfolio owner and investment manager has structured and explicit mandates and restrictions. The investment manager must follow these mandates to ensure the portfolio owner knows what to expect with regards to risk, industry or regional focus, investment style, and other important factors.

The investment manager uses expertise to build equity and strengthen the portfolio, and charges for the service of managing the investments. This is covered in more detail in the section 'FUND MANAGEMENT FEES' on page 12.

Trust is vital when entrusting someone to manage a portfolio; an individual's entire financial present and future can be at stake. To prove their expertise and integrity, delegated investment managers generally earn certifications or qualifications, such as the certified financial advisor (CFA) qualification.

Importance: There are two primary reasons a client delegates portfolio management to a portfolio manager. First, the portfolio manager may have superior investment skills. The second reason is due to economies of scale in the fund management process: buying and selling securities may be expensive for a small fund, and pooling these funds under the jurisdiction of a single portfolio manager may be more efficient. Of course, the disadvantage of delegated portfolio management is that the client needs to monitor the portfolio manager.

Example: As an individual, you could delegate your investment management to a wealth manager. If you purchase shares of a fund – or run a fund – you will delegate your investment management to a portfolio manager.

WEALTH MANAGEMENT: UBS

UBS is one organisation offering wealth management services. Take a look at how it advertises these services on its website:

Our systematic, high-quality advisory approach is structured to provide superior investment advice and solutions for your wealth.

Review, understand, propose, agree and implement: the UBS advisory approach.

Our goal is to protect your assets and grow your wealth even in difficult market conditions.

The objective of our advisory approach is to help you find the right financial solution for your situation, and to provide you with full access to our integrated global capabilities.

Our rigorous investment process filters out clear signals from the noise surrounding financial markets and allows us to present you with actionable advice on your investments.

Source: www.ubs.com/global/en/wealth_management/your_goals-our_solutions/advisory_approach.html

WEALTH MANAGEMENT: FIDELITY

Fidelity is another organisation offering wealth management services. Take a look at how it advertises these services on its website:

If you're an investor with a substantial portfolio, we offer a broad range of wealth planning products and services and can provide you with in-depth guidance to help you preserve your wealth and maximize growth potential.

Source: www.fidelity.com/wealth-management/overview

INVESTMENT MANAGEMENT (SYNONYMOUS WITH PORTFOLIO MANAGEMENT)

Definition: Investment managers specialise in structuring a portfolio to optimise the value and cash flows to meet the client's needs.

A portfolio/investment manager doesn't necessarily meet with all of his investors, but he structures a fund based on a need within the market and often matches it to his expertise within an industry, region or asset class.

Importance: For individual investors, portfolio management is the process of optimising assets.

If the individual is fortunate enough to have more money coming in than going out (in the form of consumables and loan payments), they end up with money to invest. The individual has the opportunity to manage these investments intelligently, based on his or her values and risk profile.

For institutional investors, such as companies and governments, portfolio management is the process of optimising the value of the institution's assets, providing cash when required to pay off obligations (for example, pensions) or to use for growth, and making it consistent with the institution's risk profile. A portfolio's performance determines whether institutions will continue to invest money with the portfolio manager.

Example: The following are examples of investment management, one from an individual's perspective and one from an institution's perspective.

INDIVIDUAL INVESTMENT

At Wells Fargo Private Bank, our holistic approach to wealth planning starts with your relationship manager. You and your relationship manager will draw support from a team of highly experienced specialists.

Our wealth planning process focuses on developing a clear picture of your unique needs and goals, and leads to a personalized action plan that aligns solutions with those goals.

The wealth planning process begins with a core planning review that helps enable you and your family to:

- *Identify and prioritize your most important wealth management goals and concerns.*

- *Review a net worth statement to gauge your progress toward reaching those goals.*

- *Articulate how you oversee your investments and view your personal tolerance for investment risk.*

- *Review a checklist of important estate documents, including wills, powers of attorney, living trusts, and beneficiary designations.*

From this foundational understanding, your relationship manager will coordinate a team of local specialists tailored to your unique needs and goals.

For clients with comprehensive or complex wealth planning needs, we can provide consultation on various components of your wealth plan, including:

- *Retirement and cash flow planning.*

- *Company benefits and equity compensation analysis.*

- *Risk analysis and insurance planning.*

- *Investment planning and asset allocation.*

- *Education funding analysis.*

- *Estate services and gift planning.*

- *Charitable planning.*

- *Corporate executive planning services.*

- *Business advisory services.*

Source: www.wellsfargo.com

BOB: AN INDIVIDUAL INVESTOR | SAM: A WEALTH MANAGER

Bob recently got married, bought his first house, had his first baby and was promoted in his job.

After his promotion, he realised that his bank account was starting to grow but the bank wasn't paying much in interest. He decided to set up a brokerage account to invest his savings.

Bob had a friend, Samantha, who was a broker, so he gave her a call to discuss setting up an account. Samantha asked him what his investment goals were and Bob told her it was very simple: all he wanted to do was to make more money than the bank was paying him in interest. Bob also told Samantha he wanted to invest in stocks because he had many co-workers that had made lots of money investing in the stock market.

Samantha asked to meet with Bob to discuss his investment objectives, but Bob wasn't interested in the consultation as he didn't have much time between his job and his family. Instead Bob did his own research and came up with a list of stocks that had increased in value the most in the last 12 months with the hope that they would continue to increase in value in the future. Samantha set up the account for Bob and invested as he wished, but warned him that past performance did not guarantee future performance.

Over the next 12 months some of the stocks rose as they had in the past, but many went down and others remained the same price. At the end of the 12 months, Bob's investment portfolio had actually decreased in value.

For the second year, Bob sold some stocks out of his portfolio that were not performing well and purchased stocks that he hoped would perform well based on the prior year's performance. Once again, some of the stocks that had increased in value continued to do so, whereas others decreased or remained at the same price.

At the end of the second year, Bob's portfolio was down by 10% of what he initially invested (he started out with $20,000 and now had $18,000). Not only was he not making the money that he had hoped to make, but he was making less than what the bank would have paid him in interest.

Bob was thinking he would have been better off just saving the money under his mattress. He decided it was time to meet with Samantha and discuss the best way to manage his portfolio.

INSTITUTIONAL INVESTMENT MANAGEMENT

Putnam's Active Investment Solutions

With almost 200 investment professionals, disciplined investment processes, and a blend of quantitative and fundamental research, Putnam delivers a range of long-only active alpha products for institutional investors.

Equity strategies. Putnam's equity capabilities include strategies based on style, geography, and risk. Dedicated portfolio managers and global equity analysts perform bottom-up fundamental research to evaluate key drivers of return and to identify the best investment opportunities. Sophisticated risk management tools are used to construct portfolios to meet specific risk parameters.

Fixed income strategies. Putnam's Fixed Income Group is an integrated organization of almost 80 investment professionals, organized into specialist teams that cover all sectors and subsectors of the asset class. This structure allows us to combine the extensive resources of a large organization with the agility of a small, focused manager. The group – which covers roughly 10,000 securities – has the breadth and depth to evaluate new market segments and to incorporate the best opportunities from the fixed-income universe into our strategies.

Source: www.putnam.com

Global fund management industry in 2010:
Assets under management ($ trillion)

Pension funds	Mutual funds	Insurance funds	SWFs	Private equity	Hedge funds	ETFs	Private wealth
29.9	24.7	24.6	4.2	2.6	1.8	1.3	28.6

LARGEST GLOBAL INVESTMENT MANAGEMENT CENTRES (END-2010)					
	PENSION FUNDS	INSURANCE ASSETS	MUTUAL FUNDS	TOTAL CONVENTIONAL	*SHARE* (%)
USA	17,371	6,431	11,821	35,623	45
UK	2,926	2,736	854	6,516	8
Japan	1,388	3,958	786	6,123	8
France	232	2,509	1,617	4,358	6
Germany	171	1,384	334	1,889	2
Netherlands	1,057	508	86	1,651	2
Switzerland	551	427	262	1,240	2
Other	6,241	6,681	8,939	21,861	27
Total	29,937	24,634	24,699	79,270	100

Figures ($bn) are for domestically sourced funds regardless of where they are managed. No reliable comparisons are available for total funds under management by country.

Source: TheCityUK estimates based on UBS, OECD, SwissRe and Investment Company Institute data.

Dig deeper

Learn more about these organisations' portfolio management services on their websites under wealth planning and institutional investor services.

THE FUND MANAGEMENT INDUSTRY

Definition: The management of investment portfolios by professional portfolio managers is a very large global industry. Delegated portfolio management by institutional investors includes unit trusts (mutual funds), investment trusts (closed-ended funds), investment policies (life assurance, endowment policies) and pension funds.

Importance: The IMF's *Global Financial Stability Report* estimates that global assets under management by institutional investors was around $60 trillion in 2010.

The UK is the second-largest centre of asset management in the world behind the USA, and the largest in Europe. The following table shows how different types of investment vehicles are more important in some countries than in others. For example, insurance companies are the most important investment vehicle in

Japan, Germany and France, whereas pension funds are more important in the UK and USA. In the USA, mutual funds are also relatively important.

Example: As of the end of 2009, BlackRock was the largest investment manager in the world, with Allianz the largest investment manager in Europe.

LARGEST GLOBAL INVESTMENT MANAGERS			
	ASSETS UNDER MANAGEMENT (END-2009)	MARKET	ASSETS ($BN)
1	BlackRock	USA	3,346
2	State Street Global	USA	1,911
3	Allianz Group	Germany	1,859
4	Fidelity Investments	USA	1,699
5	Vanguard Group	USA	1,509
6	AXA Group	France	1,453
7	BNP Paribas	France	1,326
8	Deutsche Bank	Germany	1,261
9	JP Morgan Chase	USA	1,253
10	Capital Group	USA	1,180
11	Bank of New York Mellon	USA	1,115
12	Credit Agricole	France	918
13	UBS	Switzerland	876
14	Goldman Sachs Group	USA	871
15	HSBC Holdings	UK	857

Source: Pension & Investments/Towers Watson

FUND MANAGEMENT FEES

Definition: Fund management companies charge an annual management fee for managing a portfolio. These fees cover the salaries and advisory costs associated with fund management, trading costs from buying and selling securities, and marketing and distribution expenses. These fees are charged as a percentage of assets under management, and are typically in the range 0.5%–2%.

Fund growth generates higher fees, but there are substantial economies of scale in fund management, and doubling the size of a fund would not be expected to double the costs. Management fees on an actively managed portfolio are higher than for passive portfolios.

Management fees are of two types: (1) an *ad valorem* fee, which is typically a percentage of the assets under management, and (2) a performance-related fee that depends on the return generated by the fund manager's performance.

For example, an *ad valorem* fee of 1% per year on a £50 million mandate – that is, £500,000 per year – would be charged to compensate the firm managing the portfolio. In addition, the performance-related element may be stated as 20% of performance above the benchmark. If the £50 million fund generates a return of 3% above its benchmark, then the performance-related fee would be £300,000. This is calculated as 20% of 3% of £50 million.

Here is how Fidelity's MoneyBuilder Growth Fund explains the calculation for its total expense ratio (TER):

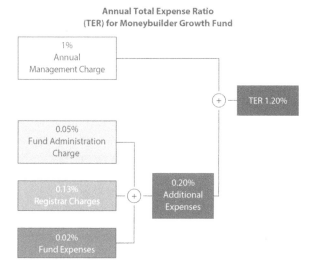

**Annual Total Expense Ratio
(TER) for Moneybuilder Growth Fund**

Importance: Money management is not free, although it has become less expensive. Investors must consider costs and understand how fees vary substantially between fund types.

Professor Kenneth R. French (2008) in his paper 'The Cost of Active Investing' reported a steady decline in the fees and expenses investors paid for mutual fund investments from 2.08% of assets under management in 1980 to 0.95% in 2006. The fees faced by institutions for fund management services were lower, having fallen from 0.34% in 1980 to 0.23% in 2006.

Institutional costs decline over time for two reasons. (1) The costs they pay for active and passive investments decline. (2) More interestingly, institutions shift a large portion of their USA equity holdings from active to passive over time.

French (2008) also reported that the average annual hedge fund fee from 1996 to 2007 was 4.26% of assets, and this was made up of the '2 and 20' performance-related fee. In fact, the average management fee is lower than this and French suggested that a better description would be '1 and 10'.

Hedge fund investors who invest in funds of funds pay two layers of fees, and the average is 6.52% per year.

Dig deeper

Read Fidelity's excellent explanation of fees: www.fidelity.co.uk/investor/research-funds/charges-fees/default.page

---

Example: Khorana, Servaes and Tufano (2008) undertook a cross-country comparison of mutual fund fees in 18 developed economies and found that fees vary substantially across funds and countries.

In 2002, the average expense ratio for equity funds worldwide was 1.29%, ranging from 1.05% in Belgium to 2.56% in Canada. They go on to assess the factors that affect these different fees and argue that fees differ due to: (a) regulatory differences and the costs of complying with particular regulations; (b) the level of competition in a particular fund management industry; (c) national economies of scale; (d) experience effects, whereby cumulative experience of the fund management industry leads to lower fees; and (e) characteristics of investors who purchase fund management services.

They find that fees are negatively related to fund size (economies of scale) and, more surprisingly, are lower in those countries where the mutual fund industry is more concentrated. Khoruna, Servaes and Tufano (2009) provide estimates of management fees around the world in 2002 based on a survey of 77,449 open-ended pooled investment vehicles (mutual funds in the USA, Undertakings for Collective Investments in Transferable Securities [UCITS] in Europe) across the countries.

They calculate these fees in three different ways. (1) Management fees (MGT) are the annual charges for management services, which include investment management services, but sometimes include administration and distribution charges. (2) TER covers management fees and also includes administration, servicing, audit and legal charges. In addition, some funds charge load factors which may be front-end or back-end, when investors purchase or redeem their investments in these funds. (3) Total shareholder costs (TSC) include the TER plus annualised loads under the assumption that the funds are held for a five-year holding period. The fees in these tables, which came from the survey, show the average fee percentages based on assets under management by country.

BONDS	MGMT	TER	TSC	TOTAL
Australia	0.61%	0.63%	0.75%	1.99%
Canada	1.44%	1.79%	1.84%	5.07%
Ireland	0.82%	1.08%	1.89%	3.79%
France	0.66%	0.85%	1.18%	2.69%
Germany	0.70%	0.79%	1.26%	2.75%
Switzerland	0.84%	0.89%	1.36%	3.09%
UK	0.79%	0.88%	1.66%	3.33%
USA	0.42%	0.78%	1.05%	2.25%

EQUITIES	MGMT	TER	TSC	TOTAL
Australia	1.09%	1.17%	1.41%	3.67%
Canada	1.96%	2.56%	3.00%	7.52%
Ireland	1.20%	1.52%	2.40%	5.12%
France	1.04%	1.22%	1.88%	4.14%
Germany	1.05%	1.17%	1.97%	4.19%
Switzerland	1.38%	1.47%	2.03%	4.88%
UK	1.07%	1.18%	2.28%	4.53%
USA	0.62%	1.11%	1.53%	3.26%

FUND PERFORMANCE AND RANKINGS

Definition: The most basic way to measure a fund's performance is to evaluate its absolute returns.

The most common fund performance measurement is the Sharpe ratio, the amount of return relative to an index. It is calculated by subtracting the benchmark return from the fund's annualised returns and dividing the result by the standard deviation of the returns.

Sharpe ratio = average (excess returns) ÷ standard deviation (excess returns)

Dig deeper

Learn more about the Sharpe ratio: web.stanford.edu/~wfsharpe/art/sr/sr.htm

Learn more about Lipper Leaders: www.lipperweb.com/Research/Leaders.aspx

---

Importance:

Fund performance

Traditionally portfolio managers were assessed in relation to a peer-group benchmark, comparing their performance against the median performance of similar funds. However, Myners (2001) reports a long-run trend away from the peer-group benchmark to customised benchmarks. This trend reflects trustees increasingly taking asset-allocation decisions on the basis of advice from consultants, and then allocating management of a class of assets to a specific portfolio manager.

The customised benchmark for that manager might then be the relevant index for that asset class. A bespoke investment management process is seen as dynamic, with the mandate evolving over time as the performance of the fund or asset class varies, and expectations of future returns change.

Fund rankings

The Lipper Leader Rating System is a toolkit that uses investor-centred criteria to deliver a simple, clear description of a fund's success in meeting certain goals, such as preserving capital, lowering expenses or building wealth. Lipper ratings provide an instant measure of a fund's success against a specific set of key metrics. These metrics can be used alone or in combination to build individualised portfolios that suit an investor's particular goals.

Example: The following two funds are managed in different ways. Fund A is focused on consistent returns, regardless of what the market does. Fund B is focused on beating the benchmark return.

FUND A	FUND RETURN	BENCHMARK RETURN	DIFFERENCE IN RETURN
2011	10%	8%	+2%
2012	10%	14%	−4%
2013	10%	4%	+6%

FUND B	FUND RETURN	BENCHMARK RETURN	DIFFERENCE IN RETURN
2011	7%	8%	−1%
2012	15%	14%	+1%
2013	5%	4%	+1%

Simple average

If you prefer absolute returns for your investment, Fund A is more appealing, especially if you prefer consistent returns year over year.

Average return: Fund A = 10% and Fund B = 9%

Standard deviation

If you prefer a fund to produce consistent returns, regardless of how the market performs, then it is best to use the standard deviation of the fund's performance.

Fund A has lower volatility, which means it has been a lower-risk asset and would be viewed as the better option if just looking at risk.

Fund A = StdDev(+10%, +10%, +10%)

Fund A = 0.00

Fund B = StdDev(+7%, +15%, +5%)

Fund B = 0.05

Sharpe ratio

If you prefer a fund that consistently outperforms the market (measured by the benchmark) with minor difference in performance compared with the market, then it is best to use the Sharpe ratio, which reveals that Fund B is more appealing.

Fund A = Average(+2%, -4%, +6%) ÷ StdDev(+2%, -4%, +6%)

Fund A = 0.0133/0.0503 = 0.2649

Fund B = Average(-1%, +1%, +1%) ÷ StdDev(-1%, +1%, +1%)

Fund B = 0.0033 ÷ 0.0115 = 0.2887

CHAPTER 3.
PORTFOLIO MANAGER'S NETWORK

OBJECTIVES

1. Introduce the network of roles involved in the portfolio management process.

2. Explain the definition and purpose of the roles in the portfolio manager's network.

PORTFOLIO MANAGER'S NETWORK

Definition: The portfolio manager's network is made up of people who provide services within his firm, within a fund administrator and within investment banks, as well as their clients. With some funds, there may also be an advisory board or a board of managers. Here we will concentrate on the core positions that contribute directly to the fund management process.

Importance: The portfolio manager is at the centre of a large network of individuals that assist with analysis, transactions, and administrative and strategic focus. This network, or team, enables the portfolio manager to function and succeed.

Example: Here is an example of a portfolio manager's network:

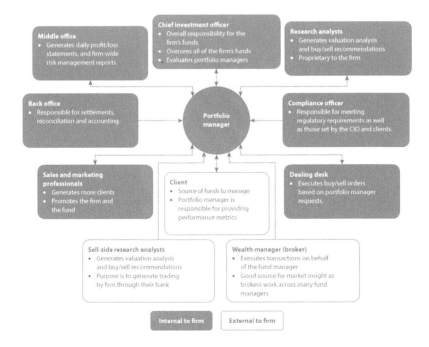

LEO: A PORTFOLIO MANAGER

Leo manages an equity fund with a medium-sized investment management firm. He has a partner and both of them focus on how to outperform their competition, which is generally noted as a 'benchmark', as well as how to attract more investors to their fund. Generally the two objectives work very well together; if they outperform their competition they will attract more investors. But that isn't always the case.

To outperform the benchmark, Leo and his partner rely on information from many sources, but it is ultimately up to them to decide where to invest. For example, Leo has research analysts that work for him to research ideas. Leo also has several friends that work for investment banks and they are always promoting their clients' stocks, sending him research reports and detailed financial analyses.

Many people refer to all this information available to a portfolio manager as a 'mosaic'. A portfolio manager uses his or her experience and knowledge of the market to interpret this information to make investment decisions.

To attract more investors, Leo and his partner pitch their performance and ideas for future investing to potential investors. As Leo wants to attract the most money for every pitch, he will present to people who can direct the most money to his fund. For example, Leo pitches his performance and ideas to Samantha as she has many wealthy clients that could be interested in his fund and she could persuade them to invest in it.

PORTFOLIO MANAGER

Definition: The portfolio manager (also known as the fund manager) oversees the portfolios and is responsible for all aspects of portfolio construction as well as the client relationship.

A portfolio manager performs a range of activities centred around investing its clients' assets. The portfolio manager manages the client's investment portfolio, with an appropriate mix of asset classes or selected assets, with the typical objective of maximising returns subject to a specified level of risk, and will adjust the portfolio over time as expectations change.

A portfolio manager generally has an MBA, Chartered Financial Advisor certification (CFA), or both.

A manager might be responsible for 'separate accounts' in which each client has his own account style and holdings. The firms where a bespoke investment approach is offered are **private management firms**. The portfolio manager might be responsible for 'pooled accounts' such as a mutual fund or hedge fund where the assets of many clients are aggregated and managed as a whole. The pooled firms are known as **investment companies**.

The portfolio manager might have a degree of client contact, particularly with larger clients, or very limited contact with clients, focusing nearly all of his time on managing the portfolio. A portfolio manager, whether from a private management firm or an investment company, will set a long-term policy style or strategy.

Portfolio managers generally specialise in a single asset class, such as fixed income or equities. Within these asset classes portfolio managers are likely to be focused on an industry, such as semiconductors or food and beverages, and possibly a region such as the USA or Europe. Individuals that manage these focused funds often come from a research analyst background, where they previously focused on analysing the same types of securities they are now managing. Broader mandates, such as a multi-asset-class strategy or a global macro hedge fund, might also be managed by someone with a research analyst background in addition to a strong quantitative background.

A key part of the portfolio manager's remit is portfolio rebalancing and performance analysis.

Importance: The role of a portfolio manager is to structure a client's portfolio, using his expertise and experience, in the expectation of maximising the assets.

The portfolio manager employs a mix of asset classes or selected assets, adjusts the portfolio through time, and provides the client with records of the portfolio's performance.

Under pooled fund management, the portfolio manager sets the long-term investment policy of the fund, and then investors such as pension funds can choose to purchase shares in this investment vehicle. Under bespoke asset management, the portfolio manager will agree a long-term policy or strategy with the pension fund that will involve specifying a relevant benchmark against which the portfolio performance will be judged.

Example: Some portfolio managers include:

- Sebastian Lyon, Troy Asset Management
- Bruce Berkowitz, Fairholme Funds
- Liu Yang, Atlantis Investment Management
- Warren Buffett, Berkshire Hathaway

Dig deeper

Learn more about fund management roles and responsibilities in Euromoney's *Global Investor Magazine*, *Asia Asset Management*, and Palgrave Macmillan's *Journal of Asset Management*.

CHIEF INVESTMENT OFFICER

Definition: The chief investment officer (CIO) is responsible for implementing the investment philosophy and policies of a company, corporation or organisation. The CIO is one of the highest-ranking executives within a financial institution, who must report to the board of trustees.

Importance: The CIO oversees the investments of all of the funds managed by the firm. He or she is responsible for the asset-allocation decisions across the firm to ensure that the firm, as a whole, is meeting its customers' needs, operating efficiently and optimising its profits.

Example: The CIOs of top firms include:

- Christopher J. Ailman, CalSTRS

- William R. Ebsworth, Fidelity's Strategic Advisors, Inc. (Individual Investors).

Dig deeper

aiCIO, an online magazine, provides great insight into the CIO's roles and responsibilities.

RESEARCH ANALYST

Definition: A research analyst researches investment opportunities, determines assets' value and makes recommendations regarding whether to buy or sell those assets.

Fundamental analyst

Fundamental analysts research a company's operating performance and project its future performance, based on assumptions on the quality of the management team, changes in the market, competitive forces, and any other industry- or region-specific events expected in the future.

With their predictions, the fundamental analyst will value the company (see the section 'EQUITY-SELECTION PROCESS' on page 90) and determine whether its stock price is above or below its true value.

Most fundamental analysts have an industry specialty (such as technology, consumer cyclical products, health care or financial institutions) as they need the expertise to make assumptions about companies' growth and market. Analysts generally gain their expertise by working in the industry or by researching and following the assets over a long time.

The fundamental analyst is responsible for presenting investment ideas to the portfolio manager. The portfolio manager then decides whether to buy a new stock or adjust the holdings of an existing stock.

Quantitative analyst

Quantitative analysts use computer-based trading systems and employ the latest investment management technology to give their analysis an edge. They develop quantitative models for portfolio management, research analysis and risk management purposes.

A successful quantitative analyst will be tech-savvy and often have programming skills. In many funds or companies, this is a hybrid job between the investment team and IT department. The quantitative analyst generally holds a degree in mathematics, economics, physics or a similar highly numerate subject, with a financial background, extensive programming knowledge and a good understanding of business needs.

Importance: All investment research analysts are critical to the portfolio manager's network as they allow the portfolio manager to consider a broader universe of assets with the analysts' assistance.

Depending on the breadth of assets that the portfolio manager has within his investible universe, it is incredibly difficult for the portfolio manager to analyse in great detail all potential investment ideas. He or she relies heavily on smart investment research analysts.

Example: Investment research analysts within a fund are generally behind the scenes and don't publicise themselves or their analysis. They are therefore not widely known.

Dig deeper

The CFA Institute's *Financial Analysts Journal* is a very good resource for learning more about financial analysts.

DEALING DESK (TRADERS)

Definition: The dealing desk, or specifically the trader on that desk within an investment management firm, is responsible for buying at the lowest price and selling at the highest price to meet the requirements of the portfolio manager.

A portfolio manager will dictate the security they would like to purchase, but it is up to the trader to use their knowledge to decide when, and at what price, to execute a trade.

Importance: After the portfolio manager decides what to buy or sell, he or she gives instructions to their traders, who then execute the actual buying and selling.

Because the trader takes and fulfills orders for the portfolio manager, dedicated traders at institutional management firms often have less discretion in their activities than traders at other types of institutions, which are focused on trading purely to make a profit within a short period.

Example: Traders are typically behind-the-scenes and don't gain much publicity within the investment firm if they do their job well. Sadly, only those traders that have done such a poor job, or have actually brought their firms to failure or into disrepute, are the ones that are well-known to the public.

Here are some examples of rogue traders:

- Nick Leeson, Barings Bank (est. loss: £827 million)
- Yasuo Hamanaka, Sumitomo Holdings (est. loss: $2.6 billion)
- Jérôme Kerviel, Société Générale (est. loss: €4.9 billion)
- Kweku Adoboli, UBS (est. loss: $2.3 billion).

Dig deeper

Traders Magazine is a good resource for traders.

Kimberly D. Krawiec published an academic paper about rogue trading:
scholarship.law.duke.edu/faculty_scholarship/2045

SALES AND MARKETING PROFESSIONALS

Definition: Sales and marketing professionals are responsible for bringing in clients who entrust their money to the firm's portfolio manager.

The process includes identifying prospective clients (e.g. corporations, government entities, foundations and endowments) and maintaining current clients by partnering with institutional clients and financial advisors who offer their firm's funds to clients through individual accounts or as part of retirement plans.

Importance: Sales and marketing professionals are responsible for maintaining an asset base for the portfolio manager to manage. Without sales and marketing, the fund may not have any assets to manage.

Example: Sales and marketing professionals will be responsible for target market and distribution channel analysis and consulting, marketing tools and communications, fund fact sheets, annual reports, informational brochures, prospectuses, newsletters, advisor promotion materials and material to help brokers promote their fund.

MIDDLE AND BACK OFFICE

Definition: The terms 'middle office' and 'back office' refer to the investment management fund professionals who support the 'front office' (the client-facing teams within banks and investment firms, such as portfolio managers, analysts and traders).

Middle and back office professionals deal with the operations and technology of the investment firm. They are concerned with such matters as ensuring the settlement of trades, that holdings are adjusted at the end of the day due to price and corporate action changes, and maintaining records of counter parties involved in the firm's transactions. This team is responsible for ensuring all systems are working and all reporting can be analysed and maintained by the front and middle office.

Importance: The middle office is responsible for identifying and managing risk, tracking financial performance of the firm, as well as ensuring the firm as a whole will continue to be viable. The compliance officer is also considered part of the middle office. The back office looks after the foundation of the operations and is responsible for many things, including ensuring the accounting and finance systems are working and that adjustments are made to portfolios based on transactions and corporate actions.

Example: A professional in the middle office might be responsible for valuation validation – i.e. where middle office will compare the valuation of each holding in a portfolio to two or more independent sources. The purpose of this is to determine whether the valuation of the holding in the portfolio is within an established tolerance range. The middle office is likely to use sophisticated valuation models to provide the portfolio manager with additional information.

A professional in the back office might be responsible for merging two stocks in the portfolio on the basis of the deal terms of the transaction and ensuring that the new price is correct and available on the day that the acquisition is effective.

Dig deeper

Securities Technology Monitor magazine covers some topics related to the middle and back office.

COMPLIANCE OFFICER

Definition: The fund compliance officer manages the regulatory affairs and other jurisdictions that may affect the fund, from a client perspective and from an investment perspective. They are responsible for general compliance – ensuring that all investment decisions comply with client and legal mandates.

This role involves ongoing compliance monitoring, reporting and reviewing. The compliance officer also revises and maintains the fund's compliance policies. He or she manages all licensing requirements and interacts on a daily basis with the portfolio managers and fund principals.

The compliance officer will probably have a strong transactional legal background: fund formation, covered employment agreements, and be able to communicate well with senior business thought leaders.

Importance: Many global exchange commissions, such as the Securities and Exchange Commission (SEC) in the USA, require funds to have an assigned chief compliance officer to adopt and implement written policies and procedures reasonably designed to prevent violation of the federal securities laws, and to review those policies and procedures annually for their adequacy and the effectiveness of their implementation.

Example: The compliance officer is generally named publicly only if things go wrong. One example is when Jon Corzine (a former CEO of Goldman Sachs) experienced excessive losses and money went missing, and people questioned whether the firm's chief compliance officer, Tracy Whille, had the right policies and procedures in place.

Dig deeper

Compliance Week is an insightful magazine for learning about the compliance officer.

J.P. Morgan's site includes a valuable article about chief compliance officers.

SELL-SIDE RESEARCH ANALYST

Definition: As with the investment research analyst at the investment management firm (known as 'the buy-side'), the 'sell-side' research analyst at the investment banks generates very similar analysis. These analysts generally focus on an industry and/or region and become experts in their domains.

Importance: The sell-side analyst's primary objective is to help drive more transactions through their bank, either directly in the form of sales and trading transactions, or indirectly in the form of merger and acquisition (M&A) transactions or equity/debt underwritings.

The analyst increases sales and trading transactions by pitching his analysis and recommendations to the investment management firms. The increased M&A transactions and equity/debt underwritings are a result of the investment bankers pitching the bank's knowledge of the industry to companies, highlighting the analyst's research and influence.

Example: There have been many notable sell-side research analysts.

- Abby Joseph Cohen, Goldman Sachs
- Henry Blodget, analyst turned blogger.

Dig deeper

Read an interesting overview of analyst roles at: www.sec.gov/investor/pubs/analysts.htm

---

WEALTH MANAGER (BROKER)

Definition: The wealth manager provides financial advice to his clients and this is important to the fund manager as the wealth manager can advise clients to purchase specific funds. The wealth manager needs to understand a fund's value and where it fits into his clients' investment requirements.

Importance: The wealth manager plays an important role for the portfolio manager, as these brokers interface directly with clients and advise them which funds to invest in. If wealth managers like a portfolio manager's fund, then more assets will be directed to the fund and the portfolio manager will earn more.

Example: Large wealth managers include Morgan Stanley, Deutsche Bank, Ameriprise, Merrill Lynch, UBS, and Lloyds.

Dig deeper

Reputable wealth management magazines include *SmartMoney* (USA), *Professional Wealth Management* (UK) and *Financial Wealth* (Asia Pacific).

SAMANTHA: A WEALTH MANAGER'S ROLE

Samantha is a wealth manager at a large financial institution. Her clients range from senior executives and professional athletes who have significant amounts of wealth to invest, down to family and friends who are budding investors looking for advice to get started, like her friend Bob.

The most important part of Samantha's job is to be a trusted advisor and to create complete transparency for her clients so they can feel comfortable with the expected outlook of their wealth. A good wealth manager is one that matches her client's objectives with the assets that will meet their needs from both a risk and a return perspective.

Samantha is compensated based on the amount of assets under management as well as commissions paid to the firm for investment in certain assets that are owned by the firm or where there is an arrangement with another firm.

Similar to Leo, Samantha pitches her skills to investors, but as she doesn't manage a portfolio, she is more reliant on customer recommendations as well as the security and reputation of the firm that employs her.

THE CLIENT

Definition: The client is a person, company, government or even another fund that would like to invest and grow its portfolio.

Importance: The client is the one whose money the portfolio manager is managing. It must be well-informed and understand how a portfolio is progressing toward its goals. If the client becomes dissatisfied for any reason, it will move its money to another fund.

Example: If you are an investor and own a fund, you are the client.

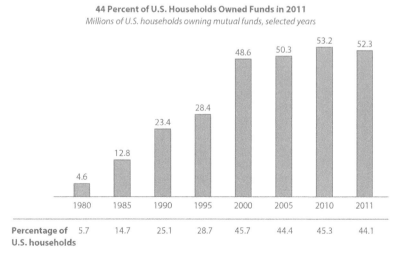

44 Percent of U.S. Households Owned Funds in 2011
Millions of U.S. households owning mutual funds, selected years

	1980	1985	1990	1995	2000	2005	2010	2011
Millions of households	4.6	12.8	23.4	28.4	48.6	50.3	53.2	52.3
Percentage of U.S. households	5.7	14.7	25.1	28.7	45.7	44.4	45.3	44.1

FUNDS AND INVESTMENTS

Whenever you find yourself on the side of the majority, it is time to pause and reflect.

Mark Twain

CHAPTER 4.
FUND TYPES

OBJECTIVES

1. **Understand different fund types.**

2. **Learn why there are different fund types.**

3. **Learn which fund types are growing in popularity and why.**

Dig deeper

Learn more about different fund types: www.fidelity.co.uk/investor/funds/
funds-explained/types-of-funds.page

INVESTMENT FUNDS

Definition: Investment funds are collective investment schemes and are of two types: open-ended and closed-ended funds. These funds can be managed actively or passively.

Note: While the term 'mutual' may refer to both types of scheme, it is more common to describe open-ended funds as mutual.

Actively managed fund: A fund where the portfolio manager makes security-selection decisions on the basis of better information or better investment skills than the market to realise a return above a benchmark.

Passively managed fund: A fund where the portfolio manager adopts a stock-selection strategy that tracks the market portfolio to an appropriate index.

Importance: Different types of investment fund have different fees, management styles and risks that you need to be aware of as part of your portfolio-selection process.

Example: Examples of investment funds are below.

	OPEN-ENDED	CLOSED-ENDED
Actively Managed	Pension Fund	Hedge Fund
Passively Managed	ETFs	

There are no closed-ended funds that are passively managed as the purpose of structuring a closed-ended fund is to actively manage a fixed amount of assets.

OPEN-ENDED INVESTMENT FUNDS

Definition: An open-ended investment fund (OEIC) or unit trust is a collective investment scheme that pools money from many investors and invests the money in stocks, bonds, short-term money market instruments or other securities.

It is open-ended because the number of 'units' in each trust varies according to supply and demand. It is collective because it puts together the money from many different investors for a professional investment manager to manage.

Investors buy and sell shares in the mutual fund from the fund itself (or through a broker), rather than through a stock exchange. The price investors pay for mutual fund shares is the fund's per share net asset value (NAV) plus any fees that the fund imposes at purchase (such as sales loads). Open-ended fund shares are 'redeemable', in that when investors want to sell their fund shares they sell them back to the fund at their approximate NAV, minus any fees the fund imposes at that time (redemption fees).

Importance: When investors buy shares in an open-ended fund, the portfolio manager uses the money given by these investors to buy additional securities, so that the size of the fund increases or decreases as investors buy and sell shares in the fund. Open-ended funds generally sell shares on a daily basis, although some funds will stop selling when, for example, they become too large.

These funds will have different investment objectives and portfolio holdings; the fund's policy statement should clearly state them. Different funds may also be subject to different risks, volatility, and fees and expenses.

Example: Open-ended funds come in many varieties. For example, there are index funds, stock funds, bond funds, money market funds and more.

Dig deeper

Learn about the details of Scottish Widows OEIC funds: www.
scottishwidows.co.uk/investments/open_ended_investment_companies/
in_detail.html

CLOSED-ENDED FUNDS

Definition: Closed-ended funds (CEFs), or investment trusts, are companies that invest in the shares of other companies. Like open-ended funds, they are collective investments which pool together the money of many investors, and this money is then invested in a portfolio of underlying securities.

Closed-ended funds sell a fixed number of shares at an initial public offering when the fund is listed on a stock exchange and these shares in the fund then trade on the stock market.

After the initial public offering, if an investor wants to buy shares in the closed-ended fund, the investor will buy from another investor who is selling. Closed-ended fund shares generally are not redeemable, that is, a closed-ended fund is not required to buy its shares back from investors.

The price of closed-ended fund shares that trade on a stock exchange will be determined by the forces of supply and demand. If lots of investors want to buy shares in a closed-ended fund, its price will rise. In this case, the share price may be above the fund's NAV: the net value of the underlying investments held by the trust. On the other hand, investment trusts may trade at a discount to their NAV.

Importance: Like open-ended funds, closed-ended funds can have different investment objectives, strategies and investment portfolios. They can also be subject to different risks, volatility, fees and expenses.

The major difference between closed-ended funds and open-ended funds is the way the cash flows in and out of the fund. When an investor sells his investment of a closed-ended fund, he sells it to another investor, not changing the amount of assets that the fund has under management. When an investor sells his investment of an open-ended fund, he sells it back to the fund, which means the fund needs to give the investor his money back, reducing the assets under management (AUM).

Example: The top five closed-ended funds for 2012 are listed in the next table.

FUND NAME (TICKER) ASSET CLASS	TOTAL NET ASSETS (MILLIONS)	1-YR MARKET RETURN
Central Fund of Canada (CEF) Sector Equity	$5,610.80	11.90%
Eaton Vance TxMgdGlDvEIn (EXG) Opt Arb/Opt Strat	$3,069.20	24.52%
Kayne Anderson MLP (KYN) Sector Equity	$2,520.80	14.15%
AllianceBernstein Income (ACG) Corp Dept BBB Lvgd	$2,300.30	11.57%
DNP Select Income Fund (DNP) Income & Pref Stk	$2,233.00	−7.95%

Source: Closed-End Fund Center

The Central Fund of Canada, traded on both the NYSE as well as the Toronto Stock Exchange, is the largest closed-ended fund traded in the USA, with $5.6 billion under management as of December 2012.

Dig deeper

The Closed-End Fund Center provides quite a lot of information about
these funds.

EXCHANGE-TRADED FUNDS

Definition: Exchange-traded funds (ETFs) are another type of open-ended
investment fund but which trade continuously on a stock market. Typically an
ETF will mimic a particular stock market index, and its investment objective will
be to achieve the same return as that market index. Exchange-traded funds
are depository receipts (like American depository receipts or ADRs), where a
financial institution buys a basket of securities mimicking a particular index and
then issues share certificates against these assets.

Importance: The ETF market has been growing rapidly owing to advantages
ETFs have over regular open-ended funds:

1. They offer more flexibility than your typical mutual fund.

2. They can be bought and sold throughout the trading day, allowing for
   intraday trading.

3. Traders have the ability to short or buy ETFs on margin.

4. Low annual management fees.

The following chart shows the growth of the ETF market from 2000 to 2010.

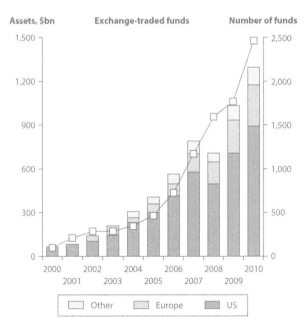

Source: BlackRock

On the other hand, there are some disadvantages of ETFs, which include:

1. commissions incurred on trading the funds

2. only institutions and the extremely wealthy can deal directly with ETF companies

3. they do not necessarily trade at the NAVs of their underlying holdings

4. there is a bid–ask spread to be paid on trading, which is an additional hidden charge.

Example: One type of ETF, known as spiders (or SPDRs), invests in all of the shares that are components of the S&P 500 Composite Stock Price Index. iShares recreate indexed positions in various global markets.

Another type of ETF includes leveraged funds that seek to achieve a daily return that is a multiple of the daily return of an index. For example, ProShares Ultra S&P 500 seeks daily investment results that correspond to twice (200%) the daily performance of the S&P 500 index.

There are also inverse ETFs, which seek to achieve an inverse multiple of the daily return of a securities index. For example, ProShares UltraShort S&P 500 seeks daily investment results that correspond to twice (200%) the inverse (opposite) of the daily performance of the S&P 500 (the index).

The following table is from ETF.com and shows the top ten ETF advisors as of 17 March 2014 based on AUM:

ISSUER	AUM ($, mm)
BlackRock	664,956.23
SSgA	380,826.68
Vanguard	345,765.32
Invesco PowerShares	101,189.40
Wisdom Tree	33,013.63
ProShares	27,370.68
Van Eck	24,670.18
Guggenheim	24,170.95
First Trust	23,800.64
Charles Schwab	18,675.60

BlackRock Fund Advisors is the largest ETF advisor, with $665 billion under management.

Dig deeper

State Street Global Advisors have set up a site (www.spdrs.com) which contains information on ETFs as well as a link to its SPDR University (www.spdru.com).

PENSION FUNDS AND INSURANCE COMPANIES

Definition: Pension funds and long-term insurance companies are sometimes called the investing institutions since they are savings vehicles which channel long-term savings into the capital markets. They accept money over long periods of time and pay this money back on the basis of specific events, such as retirement or death.

Pension schemes may be unfunded or funded. In an unfunded, pay-as-you-go scheme, the pension represents a transfer made from the current working population to the current retired population. In a funded scheme, contributions are made into a pension fund which, during the accumulation phase, grows in value up to retirement. After retirement, the fund enters the decumulation phase and pays out a pension to the retired pensioners for the remainder of their lives.

Individual pension schemes are always funded and pay a pension at retirement on a defined contribution basis. This means that the individual receives a pension that depends on the accumulated assets in the fund. Personal pensions in the UK and 401(k) pension plans or individual retirement accounts (IRAs) in the USA are examples of such schemes and are generally structured as 'defined contribution', where individuals have some choice over the type of investments in the fund. Under defined contribution pensions, the pensioner bears the risk of fund underperformance.

Individual pension schemes that have delegated investment management will typically be constituted on a pooled basis, operated by an insurance company. The type of fund management chosen for occupational pension schemes will depend in part on the advice given by consultant actuaries, who assess the financial viability of the occupational pension scheme.

Under an insured scheme, contributions are made into a pooled vehicle, which guarantees to pay a predefined benefit at a predefined time. The risk of a funding shortfall (ignoring default risk) is borne by the portfolio manager (typically an insurance company), and not the individual or the corporation. Most small schemes will be run as insured fund management. Under a self-administered scheme, where the pension fund sponsors have some control over the investment management, fund management may be outsourced to one or more external managers, or managed in-house.

Very large funded pension schemes are typically managed by a team of in-house professionals, allowing complete flexibility in terms of asset/liability matching. However, the risk of a contribution shortfall lies solely with the scheme sponsor.

Importance: Insurance company and pension fund assets as a percentage of gross domestic product (GDP) have been increasing in most major developed countries over the past ten years as seen in the following two charts. In the USA, UK and France, the combined amount of assets managed by insurance companies and pension funds exceeds annual GDP.

Example: The next table is a list of the largest insurance companies by market capitalisation as of November 2011. The list excludes Berkshire Hathaway. While it is classified as an insurance company as that was the foundation of its AUM, it has evolved into more of an investment fund.

LARGEST INSURANCE COMPANIES BY MARKET CAP			
RANK	**COMPANY**	**MARKET CAP USD (MIL)**	**COUNTRY**
1	China Life Insurance Company Limited	75,563	China
2	Ping An Insurance (Grp) Co of China Ltd.	48,691	China
3	Allianz SE	44,151	Germany
4	American International Group, Inc.	41,555	United States
5	AIA Group Ltd	35,643	Hong Kong
6	MetLife, Inc.	32,385	United States
7	Zurich Financial Services	31,856	Switzerland
8	AXA	29,699	France
9	ING Groep N.V.	26,001	Netherlands
10	China Pacific Insurance (Group) Co., Ltd	25,721	China

Source: Thomson Reuters (as of 22 November 2011)

HEDGE FUNDS

Definition: A hedge fund is effectively an unregulated investment pool which may invest in a variety of assets. According to some estimates they have grown in number from as few as 300 in 1990 to anything up to 5,000 today, managing nearly $2 trillion of funds worldwide.

Because they are free from regulatory and disclosure requirements hedge funds can be extremely flexible in their investment options and change their portfolios faster than larger regulated vehicles.

Hedge fund investing originally involved managers taking positions in individual securities which were either long or short on the basis of their views on the valuation of that security. Because these funds took long and short positions in individual securities, they were able to 'hedge' market risk. But over the years, the term 'hedge fund' has come to encompass a wide variety of alternative investment strategies.

Here is a list of a number of typical hedge fund strategies:

- trading strategies (based on speculation about market direction in multiple asset classes)

- relative value strategies – arbitrage – focused on the spread relationships between pricing components of financial assets (may involve minimal market risk but often requires leverage to enhance returns)

- specialist credit strategies (involves lending to credit-sensitive issuers, for example, firms in or near bankruptcy, following a high level of due diligence work identifying mispriced securities, vulture funds, distressed securities investing)

- stock selection (combinations of long and short positions, normally in equities, aiming to exploit under and overvalued securities, such as pairs trading which is market neutral)

- funds of funds, which allows smaller investors to invest in hedge funds (this is when funds invest in a number of other hedge funds, and sell shares to the public).

Hedge funds tend to target significantly higher returns than funds managed in a more conventional manner. A number of factors may help them to do so:

1. They are focused on their own areas of expertise, tending to avoid risks outside those areas.

2. They operate on a performance-fee structure which, it is argued, attracts successful managers and incentivises them.

3. Hedge fund managers will often have their own money invested in the fund. A standard hedge fund fee structure would be (2:20) meaning annual management fee of 2% of AUM plus 20% of excess returns above an agreed benchmark.

Hedge Fund Industry
Assets Under Management—Historical Growth of Assets

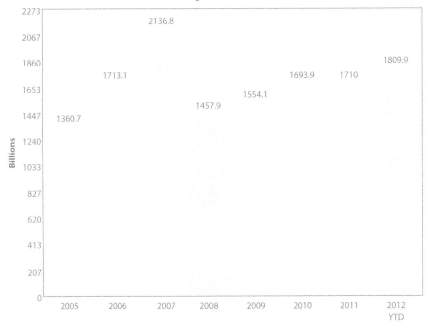

Source: www.barclayhedge.com (as of December 2012)

Moreover, there tends to be very little correlation between the performance of one type of hedge fund and another (in contrast to conventional investment funds), and between most hedge funds and market indices. Investment in one or more hedge funds (or a carefully constructed fund of funds) can therefore generate superior risk-adjusted returns, which are uncorrelated with the remainder of a typical institutional investor's portfolio. However, the selection of funds is crucial, and must take place on the basis of careful research, since – as is also true of private equity funds – the dispersion of returns for hedge funds is much wider than for conventional active management, as are the sources of competitive advantage, risk and return.

Importance: The hedge fund industry currently has about $1.8 billion AUM and has been growing since taking a large drop in 2008.

Historically, institutional investors have been cautious about hedge fund investing, with high-net-worth individuals providing the primary client-base for most hedge funds. This reticence stems from a limited understanding of the different styles of hedge fund and the risk diversification and return enhancement potential they can provide. It also arises from the fact that fees tend to be high and charged on a performance basis, and the positions taken by a hedge fund manager are likely to be significantly different to the consensus – a very different set of characteristics to those with which many institutional investors tend to be comfortable. Moreover, there are significant capacity constraints, with some high-profile funds closing to investors very soon after opening.

Example: At the time of writing, the largest hedge fund is Bridgewater, run by Ray Dalio. You can read more about the fund and its investment style on its website.

PRIVATE EQUITY AND VENTURE CAPITAL FUNDS

Definition: Private equity is an ownership share in a company that is not traded on a public stock exchange, but may be traded on a private stock exchange, such as the Private Equity Exchange (www.peqx.com). It is a way to buy and sell shares, but is less transparent than public exchanges and does not guarantee the ability to buy or sell shares. In contrast, public equity is an ownership share of a company that is listed on a stock exchange, such as the NYSE, NASDAQ or FTSE, so the shares can be easily bought or sold. There are several types of private equity investor, but the main ones can be categorised as angel investors, venture capitalists and private equity firms.

Angel investors are those individuals that have a passion for helping to form a brand new company. These individuals may be friends or family of an entrepreneur who believe the individual will be successful with his or her idea, no matter what form the company actually takes. These investors can also be wealthy individuals who like to work with start-ups and share their expertise and provide funding for a piece of the company. There are many different angel investor networks all over the world that help to bring together entrepreneurs and angel investors.

Angel investors are focused on the seed stage of a company's capital-raising. The seed stage is an equity investment to allow a business concept to be developed, perhaps involving the production of a business plan, prototypes and additional research prior to bringing a product to market.

Venture capitalists are financial intermediaries who raise funds from institutions and investors and invest the funds in a portfolio of private companies. Venture investment is focused on growing companies to the point where a company goes public or is acquired by a larger company – the exit strategy for the investor. In order to best achieve an exit, venture capitalists will focus on those companies where they feel the market will be most successful and will work closely with their portfolio companies to ensure investment capital is put to best use. The most successful venture capitalists generally have experience working in markets where their portfolio companies are focused and they can provide guidance, expertise and a list of contacts to increase the probability of success.

Venture capitalists are primarily focused on the start-up and expansion stages of a company. At the start-up stage of a company, an investment is focused on developing a company's product, initiating scalable manufacturing, and building out of the sales and marketing functions.

The expansion stage is when the company has successfully proven its business model and is functioning across its departments, but needs investment capital to expand beyond its current capabilities. This capital will be used to expand into new markets or regions or to grow very quickly in an emerging sector.

Seed stage: The seed stage is an equity investment to allow a business concept to be developed, perhaps involving the production of a business plan, prototypes and additional research, prior to bringing a product to market and commencing large-scale manufacturing.

Only a few seed financings are undertaken each year by venture capital firms. Many seed financings are too small and require too much hands-on support from a private equity firm to make them economically viable as investments.

There are also specialist private equity firms, which, subject to a company meeting their investment preferences, provide seed capital. Business angels provide capital too, with the business angel joining a company's board, and these may be more attractive to private equity firms when later-stage funds are required.

Start-up stage: The start-up stage is an equity investment to develop a company's products, initiate commercial manufacturing and fund their initial marketing. Companies may be in the process of being set up or may have been trading for a short time, but not have sold their product commercially. Although many start-ups are typically smaller companies, there are an increasing number of multi-million dollar start-ups.

Expansion stage: The expansion stage is an equity investment to enable an established company to grow and expand. Uses of proceeds from these investments include increasing production capacity, product development, marketing, or providing additional working capital (also known as 'development' or 'growth' capital). This stage is associated with private equity rather than pure venture capital.

Other stages of private equity include: management buy-outs (MBOs), where the current operating management is provided with funds to acquire a significant shareholding in the business it manages, and management buy-ins (MBIs), where a management team from outside a company buys into it.

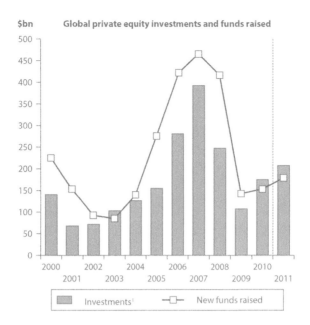

$bn   **Global private equity investments and funds raised**

¹*equity value of deals*

Source: TheCityUK estimates

Importance: The AUM of private equity and venture capital funds fluctuates significantly based on many factors in the market. As these investments are much less liquid than others, there is greater risk investing in these funds. On the flip-side, with greater risk there is also a greater opportunity for significant returns compared with other funds. As you can see in this chart, 2001 was a significant low, with just over $50 billion under management. By 2007, the amount increased to about $400 billion, before dropping significantly again.

Example: Kleiner Perkins Caufield & Byers (KPCB) and 3i are two successful and well-known private equity and venture capital funds.

SOVEREIGN WEALTH FUNDS

Definition: Sovereign wealth funds (SWFs) are a relatively recent investment vehicle. They are state-owned pools of money derived from a country's reserves, which may be supplied by the central bank or from revenues generated, for example, from the export of natural resources such as oil.

Typically, a SWF is held on a trust basis to benefit the citizens of its country. SWFs are created when a country has been running a balance of payments surplus: governments with budgetary surpluses and little international debt.

The majority of SWFs are funded by state-owned oil and gas-related reserves. The states are not required to disclose their holdings or investments, so it is difficult to determine how the funds are invested.

Importance: The estimated AUM by SWFs is $2.7 trillion as of the end of 2011, based on GeoEconomica's report 'Global Sovereign Wealth Funds Increase Assets Under Management'.

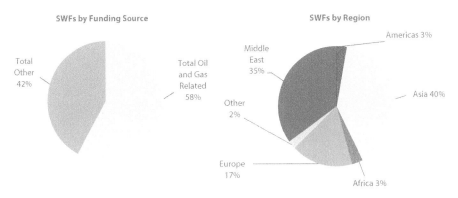

SWFs by Funding Source

Total Other 42%

Total Oil and Gas Related 58%

SWFs by Region

Americas 3%

Middle East 35%

Other 2%

Asia 40%

Europe 17%

Africa 3%

Source: Sovereign Wealth Fund Institute (www.swfinstitute.org)

Example: This table shows the top ten SWFs based on AUM.

COUNTRY	SOVEREIGN WEALTH FUND NAME	ASSETS $BILLION	INCEPTION	ORIGIN
Norway	Government Pension Fund-Global	$664.3	1990	Oil
UAE-Abu Dhabi	Abu Dhabi Investment Authority	$627	1976	Oil
China	SAFE Investment Company	$567.9**	1997	Non-Commodity
Saudi Arabia	SAMA Foreign Holdings	$532.8	n/a	Oil
China	China Investment Corporation	$482	2007	Non-Commodity
China-Hong Kong	Hong Kong Monetary Authority Investment Portfolio	$298.7	1993	Non-Commodity
Kuwait	Kuwait Investment Authority	$296	1953	Oil
Singapore	Government of Singapore Investment Corporation	$247.5	1981	Non-Commodity
Singapore	Temasek Holdings	$157.5	1974	Non-Commodity
Russia	National Welfare Fund	$149.7*	2008	Oil

Australia's Future Fund is an example of an SWF, with approximately $80 billion under management as of September 2012. The Future Fund was established by the Future Fund Act 2006 to help future Australian governments meet the cost of public sector superannuation liabilities by delivering investment returns on contributions to the fund.

Dig deeper

Learn more about SWFs and the industry at the SWF Institute's site: www. swfinstitute.org

---

LEO: A MEMBER OF THE FUND COMMUNITY

Leo manages an open-ended investment fund and, since one of his main objectives is to attract investors to his fund, he pitches his performance and his ideas to other funds to encourage them to invest. It is actually very common for certain funds to invest in other funds. For example, pension funds, insurance companies and SWFs may invest in other funds to tap into other fund managers' investment skills or expertise in a certain region or sector.

With other funds, not only will Leo present his performance and investment ideas, he will also explain how his investment style fits with the investment styles of the larger funds. If one of the SWFs has strict rules about the types of company it won't invest in, Leo needs to highlight that he screens those out of his potential investments. For example, some funds refuse to invest in companies that produce weapons, alcohol, tobacco or other products or services that cause people to deem them 'sin stocks'. Leo will show the funds how he avoids investing in these companies.

In addition to promoting his fund, Leo is always building his network with other fund managers to learn about what others in the industry are thinking and where they see opportunities and risk. The fund management industry experiences a lot of movement of employees, as fund managers with strong skills are often recruited by larger funds, so it is always good for Leo to build his network within this community.

CHAPTER 5.
INVESTIBLE UNIVERSE

OBJECTIVES

1. Introduce the most common asset types in an investment fund's portfolio.

2. Learn how the asset types vary based on risk.

3. Consider which assets might best fit your portfolio.

INVESTIBLE UNIVERSE

Definition: The investible universe is the entire scope of assets a portfolio manager will analyse to determine which specific assets will be included in his fund.

This universe is stated within the fund's prospectus and can be limited by many factors or none at all. Funds often limit their investment universe to an asset class, geography or industry; the choice is generally based on the expertise of the portfolio manager.

Importance: It is important for a portfolio manager to define his investible universe to determine where he will focus his analysis and seek opportunities to outperform the market.

A fund may focus on investments across all asset types, but expertise in a few areas help the portfolio manager's network to analyse and manage the investments more successfully.

Defining the investible universe ensures the risk characteristics of the assets within the universe match the objectives of the investors. A fund designed to retain its value will probably want to avoid volatile assets, while a fund designed to provide income back to its investors may want to avoid illiquid investments.

LEO: HIS FUND'S INVESTIBLE UNIVERSE

Leo's fund is a US equity technology fund focused on semiconductor companies. He is incredibly knowledgeable about the semiconductor industry and stays abreast of all of the companies in this industry, whether

---

they are traded in the USA or elsewhere. He also has to maintain a good understanding of emerging technologies and developments with the smaller private companies in the industry.

Even with all of this work, Leo's investible universe is focused on technology companies that trade on US exchanges. He has also stated in his prospectus that he won't invest in companies with less than $100 million market capitalisation, which means he won't invest in the smallest public companies.

The defined investible universe is helpful on three fronts. Firstly, it lets the investors that invest in Leo's fund know exactly in what types of company he will invest their money. This is helpful as an investor may have an investment strategy where they want a certain percentage of their investments in a market or industry. Secondly, it ensures Leo stays focused on a narrow slice of all of the stocks available. As he has a relatively small team, investors want to ensure he doesn't chase after every whim he may have. Thirdly, and probably most importantly, it allows the investors to measure Leo's performance relative to a benchmark. At the end of the year, they will be able to measure Leo's performance against an index of US semiconductor stocks.

The following table lists the most common asset types and the risk criteria a portfolio manager will consider when determining whether they should be included in the investible universe.

	EXAMPLES	RISK
Money Market	Treasury Bills, Currencies	Lowest due to liquidity
Bonds	Corporate Bonds, Government Bonds	Lower due to fixed income and seniority
Equity	Preferred Shares, Common Stock	Higher due to business risk and lower seniority
Derivatives	Options, Futures, Swaps	High due to volatility
Alternative Investments	Venture Capital, Hedge Funds	High due to illiquidity

Example: An example of a fund with a narrowly focused investment universe is the FundSmith Equity Fund, which has approximately $450 million under management and only invests in equities.

An example of a fund that invests in a very diverse investment universe is the Harvard Endowment Fund, which has over $30 billion under management and invests in all types of asset, including buying up tree farms.

Dig deeper

The New York Stock Exchange (NYSE) Arca Tech 100 Index clearly explains its investible universe in the 'Index Composition' section of its prospectus. The equity-focused, strict criteria helps screen out companies and asset types for greater success.

MONEY MARKET

Definition: The money market is short-term debt and monetary instruments that mature in less than one year and are very liquid.

These markets are described as 'money markets' because the assets that are bought and sold are short term – with maturities ranging from one day to one year – and normally are easily convertible into cash. Money markets include markets for such instruments as bank accounts, including term certificates of deposit; interbank loans (loans between banks); money market mutual funds; commercial paper; Treasury bills; and securities lending and repurchase agreements (repos). These assets can be bought and sold directly from a bank.

Importance: These markets comprise a large share of the financial system – in the United States, accounting for about one-third of all credit, according to the Federal Reserve Board's flow of funds survey.

Example: Treasury bills, which are issued by the government, are securities with maturities of less than a year. US Treasury bills, sold at a discount from face value and actively bought and sold after they are issued, are the safest instrument in which to place short-term savings.

The markets are deep and liquid, and trading is covered by securities laws. US Treasury bills are not only savings instruments; they can be used to settle transactions. Treasury bills, which are issued electronically, can be sent through the payments system as readily as money.

Dig deeper

Read the International Monetary Fund's excellent explanation of the money market in its article, 'What are Money Markets?', written by Randall Dodd, a financial economist at the US Treasury Department: www.imf.org/external/pubs/ft/fandd/2012/06/basics.htm

BONDS

Definition: Bonds are financial obligations from a borrower to a lender. The majority of bonds are issued by governments and corporations.

Governments and companies raise money to (a) expand operations, (b) finance deficits, (c) enhance fiscal discipline, and (d) restructure the existing debt stock of short-term debt to longer-term obligations.

Investors in bonds can purchase them at time of issuance or at a later date in the secondary market. Although some bonds are traded publicly through exchanges, most trade over the counter between large broker-dealers acting on their clients' or their own behalf.

GOVERNMENT BONDS

The government bond sector is a broad category, but the most common are those bonds that are issued and backed by a central government. Examples of these bonds are Government of Canada Bonds (GoCs), UK Gilts, US Treasuries, German Bunds (German for bonds), Japanese Government Bonds (JGBs), and Brazilian Government Bonds. The USA, Japan and Europe have historically been the biggest issuers in the government bond market.

Central governments issue bonds to pursue various goals, such as supporting affordable housing or developing small businesses through agencies, a number of which issue bonds to support their operations. Some agency bonds are guaranteed by the central government while others are not. Supranational organisations, like the World Bank and the European Investment Bank, also borrow in the bond market to finance public projects and/or development.

Local governments, whether provinces, states or cities, also borrow to finance a variety of projects, from bridges to schools, as well as general operations. The market for local government bonds is well-established in the USA, where these bonds are known as municipal bonds (munis).

European local government bond issuance has grown significantly in recent years. In the USA, municipal bonds generally enjoy a tax advantage over other bonds because interest on many municipal bonds is exempt from federal taxes, and when states issue bonds, interest may be tax-exempt for state residents.

CORPORATE BONDS

Corporate bonds have historically been the largest segment of the bond market. Corporations borrow money in the bond market to expand operations or fund new business ventures. The corporate sector is evolving rapidly, particularly in Europe and many developing countries.

Corporate bonds fall into two broad categories: investment-grade and speculative-grade (also known as high-yield or 'junk') bonds. Speculative-grade bonds are issued by companies perceived to have lower credit quality and higher default risk than more highly rated, investment-grade companies. Within these two broad categories, corporate bonds have a wide range of ratings, reflecting the fact that the financial health of issuers can vary significantly.

Speculative-grade bonds tend to be issued by newer companies, companies in particularly competitive or volatile sectors, or companies with troubling fundamentals. While a speculative-grade credit rating indicates a higher default probability, higher coupons on these bonds aim to compensate investors for the higher risk. Ratings can be downgraded if the credit quality of the issuer deteriorates, or upgraded if fundamentals improve.

Importance: The bond market is by far the largest securities market in the world, providing investors with virtually limitless investment options. Many investors are familiar with this market, but as the number of new products grows, even a bond expert is challenged to keep pace. Once viewed as a means of earning interest while preserving capital, bonds have evolved into a $90 trillion global marketplace that can offer many potential benefits to investment portfolios, including attractive returns.

Governments issued bonds more frequently in the early 20th century, giving rise to the modern bond market. Investors have purchased bonds for several reasons: capital preservation, income, diversification, and as a potential hedge against economic weakness or deflation.

When the bond market became larger and more diverse in the 1970s and 1980s, bonds began to undergo greater and more frequent price changes and many investors began to trade bonds, taking advantage of another potential benefit: price, or capital, appreciation. Today, investors may choose to buy bonds for any or all of these reasons.

Source: www.pimco.com/en/education/pages/everythingyouneedtoknowaboutbonds.aspx

Example: A commonly used example of government bonds are US Treasury bonds as they are considered risk-free and the US government issues a lot of bonds. A good way of viewing bonds is in a yield curve as displayed in this section. The yield curve shows the different yields of the bonds based on the time that the bond expires (time to maturity), which is when the government will pay back the face value of the bond.

In the chart you will see that the later the government will pay back the bond, the higher the yield. This means that if you purchase a bond that won't be paid back for 30 years, you will receive a higher yield than if you purchase a bond that will be paid back in one year. The reason for the higher yield is that there are more risks associated with lending money for a longer period of time (see chapter 7 for more details).

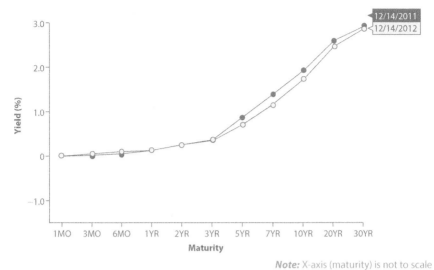

Note: X-axis (maturity) is not to scale

Source: US Treasury (www.treasury.gov)

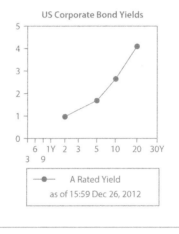

Dig deeper

Read the Australian Securities & Investments Commission's (ASIC)
interesting paper, 'Investing in Corporate Bonds?': www.moneysmart.gov.
au/media/132057/investing-in-corporate-bonds.pdf

EQUITY

Definition: An equity instrument signifies: (a) an ownership position in a corporation and (b) a claim on its proportional share in the corporation's assets and profits.

This equity is generally represented by stock. Most stocks provide voting rights, which give shareholders a proportional vote in certain corporate decisions (such as the election of corporate directors, corporate restructuring, and acquisitions).

Equity funds refer to public equity, the stocks that can be bought and sold on stock exchanges where there are controls and monitoring in place by an exchange commission. In the USA, the largest exchanges are the NYSE and NASDAQ, both of which are controlled and monitored by the Securities and Exchange Commission (SEC).

Importance: At the end of 2012, there were 46,325 companies that traded on stock exchanges across the world with the market value of $52.7 trillion for these stocks. The following table shows the breakdown of market value across the world.

TIME ZONE	USD BN END-2011
Americas	19 789
Asia-Pacific	14 670
Europe Africa Middle East	12 942
Total WFE	*47 401*

Source: www.world-exchanges.org/statistics/monthly-reports

Example: The following table lists the largest publicly-traded companies in the world based on market value.

COMPANY	COUNTRY	SALES	PROFITS	ASSETS	VALUE
Apple	United States	$127.8 B	$33 B	$138.7 B	$546 B
ExxonMobil Exxon Mobil	United States	$433.5 B	$41.1 B	$331.1 B	$407.4 B
PetroChina	China	$310.1 B	$20.6 B	$304.7 B	$294.7 B
Microsoft	United States	$72.1 B	$23.5 B	$112.2 B	$273.5 B
IBM	United States	$106.9 B	$15.9 B	$116.4 B	$238.7 B
ICBC	China	$82.6 B	$25.1 B	$2,039.1 B	$237.4 B
Royal Dutch Shell	Netherlands	$470.2 B	$30.9 B	$340.5 B	$227.6 B
Chevron	United States	$236.3 B	$26.9 B	$209.5 B	$218 B
China Mobile	Hong Kong-China	$81.7 B	$19.5 B	$151.2 B	$216.5 B
General Electric	United States	$147.3 B	$14.2 B	$717.2 B	$213.7 B

Source: Forbes Global 2000 for 2012

Dig deeper

You can learn more about a specific company's stock by researching their site. Here are a few popular companies to get started with:

www.google.com/finance

finance.yahoo.com

www.reuters.com/finance

DERIVATIVES

Definition: Derivatives are financial instruments linked to a specific financial instrument, indicator or commodity. Specific financial risks can be traded in markets through derivatives.

Derivatives are traded either on a stock exchange or in an over-the-counter (OTC) market. Derivatives traded OTC are not regulated in terms of their features and contractual provisions.

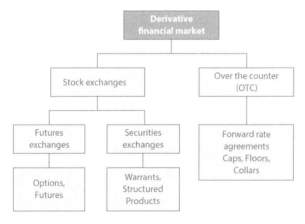

Source: www.six-swiss-exchange.com/knowhow/exchange/financial_market/derivative_market_en.html

Importance: Businesses around the world use derivatives to effectively hedge risks and reduce uncertainty about future prices. The future prices for a company's goods and services can be affected by changes in exchange rates, interest rates and commodity prices. The market's size is estimated to be over $1.2 quadrillion, but the exact amount is difficult to predict as derivatives can be easily created as they are not based on physical assets but 'derived' from prices of assets (hence the name).

Derivatives can also be used for pure profit-taking speculation. It is in this capacity that they are most commonly identified in the press, as occasionally the profits turn into extreme losses.

Example: One company is in the business of growing, harvesting, roasting and selling coffee beans. Another company is in the business of selling coffee drinks and products around the world. A coffee derivative is currently trading at $100 for one coffee contract.

If the company that sells coffee in its stores is happy with the current price, it will be able to purchase roasted beans, but it will need to purchase more in four months. To lock in the current price of the coffee beans, it buys coffee derivatives. What this means is that the coffee store will be compensated if the coffee derivatives increase in price. For example, a 25% increase in the current price will result in a 25% increase in value of the coffee store's derivatives. To ensure the coffee store is adequately covered, it will buy these derivatives to the quantity that will allow it to profit based on today's price.

If the company that grows the beans is happy with the current price, it will be able to sell its roasted beans to the market, but the market price is based on its ability to sell them today. As its crop won't be ready for sale for four months, it wants to lock in the current price by selling the coffee contract derivatives. What this means is the producer will be compensated if the price of the coffee derivative drops. For example, a 25% reduction in the current price for coffee beans will translate into a 25% increase in value of the producer's derivatives. To ensure the producer is adequately covered, it will sell these derivatives to the quantity that will allow it to profit based on today's price.

Dig deeper

Learn more about derivatives at the International Monetary Fund's site, Deutsche Borse Group's derivatives market site and its white paper, 'The Global Derivatives Market', as well as the Swiss Exchange's derivative financial market site.

ALTERNATIVE INVESTMENTS

Definition: Alternative investments are assets that aren't considered traditional investments like stocks and bonds. Typically, alternative investments have been private equity (including venture capital), real estate and commodities, but the definition is occasionally expanded to include hedge funds and funds of funds (FoFs), with the idea that these funds will likely invest in alternative investments as part of their investment strategies.

Alternative assets are not as easily bought and sold as the asset types previously mentioned; they are more illiquid and are therefore purchased with a longer-term investment horizon in mind. As these assets aren't as liquid, their value is more difficult to estimate than assets traded in a public market.

Importance: Deutsche Bank estimated that the AUM of alternative investments increased by $140 billion in 2012, taking the industry to an all-time high of $2.26 trillion.

Example: An example of a private equity fund is KKR Financial Holdings. KKR is actually a publicly-traded company, which allows investors to purchase shares of the company and own a percentage of the private company portfolio. This is unique as it allows investors to invest in KKR's portfolio of alternative investments and enjoy the liquidity of the shares being traded on a public market.

An example of a real estate fund is CBRE Group, which is also a publicly-traded fund where investors can purchase shares in the fund and own a portion of CBRE's real estate portfolio. You can get a glimpse into its investment criteria and some sample properties the fund holds by visiting its web site.

An example of a commodities fund is BHP Billiton, which is a publicly-traded mining company that allows investors to purchase shares in the company so as to own portions of its portfolio of commodities all over the world. BHP Billiton is the largest producer of commodities in the world.

Dig deeper

Read peHUB's overview of the private equity and venture capital industry.

Read Deutsche Bank's report on investors' desire to purchase 'real assets', or real estate and commodities.

OBJECTIVES, RISKS AND PHILOSOPHIES

3

Times and conditions change so rapidly that we must keep our aim constantly focused on the future.

Walt Disney

CHAPTER 6.
INVESTMENT OBJECTIVES

OBJECTIVES

1. Introduce the concept of investment objectives.

2. Introduce the investment policy statement and its purpose.

3. Encourage you to think about your own requirements with regards to investment goals, risks and performance.

INVESTMENT OBJECTIVES

Definition: It can be overwhelming for a portfolio manager to look at the universe of investible assets and the many different options for investments. Even if the portfolio manager limits the scope to public companies, there are still approximately 50,000 publicly-traded stocks to choose from around the globe.

As a portfolio manager, you need to select a universe of assets to focus on so as to become an expert in that domain. Doing so allows you to make more informed decisions based on experience and insight, instead of selecting assets just on historical performance or expected returns. To narrow the massive universe of investible assets to a manageable number, it is necessary to define investment objectives.

To define a fund's investment objectives, the portfolio manager needs to bear in mind several factors. Broadly, these factors are the fund's cash flow requirements, performance benchmark and risk-and-reward profile.

BOB: UNDERSTANDING THE NEED FOR INVESTMENT OBJECTIVES

Bob called up Samantha to tell her he was very frustrated with the performance of his portfolio. Samantha reminded him that she had wanted to sit down with him to discuss his investment objectives, but Bob hadn't had time. She also told him that his stock selections hadn't been that bad. She explained that the stock market as a whole was down over 10% and Bob should be pleased with his performance – he actually outperformed the equity market.

Of course, this doesn't make Bob feel all that great: he had been hoping to outperform what he would have received if he'd left the money in the bank.

Samantha and Bob finally sit down and discuss his goals and the need for money in the future. Bob will have to purchase a new car soon as his old one is breaking down, there are some significant repairs he will need to make to his house, and he and his wife dream about increasing the size of their home as their family expands. Also, he will need to think about paying for his kids' university costs some day, and even further out he will need to save for retirement.

Bob was thinking that if his investments outperformed what the bank was paying him in interest, all the above needs or wants would naturally fall into place. If Bob and Samantha had discussed Bob's objectives earlier, they would have designed a different portfolio, one that was balanced with less-risky assets.

Importance: Defining investment objectives is perhaps the most important step for a portfolio manager – it is the reason for the investments. For example, if the objective is to preserve capital and avoid risk, the portfolio of assets will probably be constructed with less volatile assets.

Example: The Australian Sovereign Wealth Fund – the Future Fund – has defined its investment objectives in several sections of its 'Statement of Investment Policies'.

INVESTMENT POLICY STATEMENT

Definition: An investment policy statement (IPS) serves as a strategic guide in the planning and implementation of an investment programme. The IPS is a highly customised document that is uniquely tailored to each investor's unique preferences, attitudes and situation.

Importance: When implemented successfully, the IPS anticipates issues related to governance of the investment programme, planning for appropriate asset allocation, implementing an investment programme with internal and/or external managers, monitoring the results, risk management and appropriate reporting.

The IPS also establishes accountability for the various entities that may work on behalf of an investor. Perhaps most importantly, the IPS serves as a policy guide that can offer an objective course of action to be followed during periods of market disruption when emotional or instinctive responses might otherwise prompt less-prudent actions.

Example: A good example is Putnam's IPS checklist and sample.

Dig deeper

Read the CFA Institute's brief overview of investment objectives, 'Defining Your Investment Objectives': www.cfainstitute.org/learning/investor/ Documents/defining_investment_objectives.pdf

---

CASH FLOW REQUIREMENTS

Definition: Cash flow requirements are determined by the expected need for cash payments from a fund. As an individual, managing your own fund, such cash payments may be known future expenses, such as buying a house or paying for a child's education. As an institutional portfolio manager, the cash payments may be related to pensions to be paid to retiring individuals, or agreed dividend payments to investors in your fund.

In addition to expected payments, cash flow requirements also need to cover potential unforeseen payments from the fund, such as may be necessary in the event of a job loss, where funds invested may need to be accessed to cover living expenses. A portfolio manager for an insurance company will need to consider potential events or disasters, where payments will need to be made in the short term.

Importance: Cash flow requirements will define the asset types that a portfolio manager will invest in as there will be different requirements that need to be met. If the fund is investing for the long term and there are no cash requirements, the portfolio manager can select assets that are riskier but are likely to perform better over the long term. If the fund has short-term cash requirements, the portfolio manager will need to invest in less-risky assets that will retain their value and generate fixed income for the fund.

Example: Looking at the Bank of England's pension fund update for its employees, the bank states:

> [The] objective is to manage the portfolio to maximise the likelihood that the Fund will be adequate to meet its liabilities in all future economic and financial conditions.
>
> The pie chart [below] shows how the Fund's assets were invested as at 28 February 2011.
>
> There has been hardly any change to the investment portfolio during the year. As the Fund matures, there is an increasing requirement for higher cash flow, particularly due to an increasing pensions payroll.

Due to the Bank of England's increasing requirements for cash payments to its retirees, it is essentially holding all of its investments in UK index-linked bonds, which are likely less risky and volatile than stocks.

Spread of assets at 28 February 2011 (%)

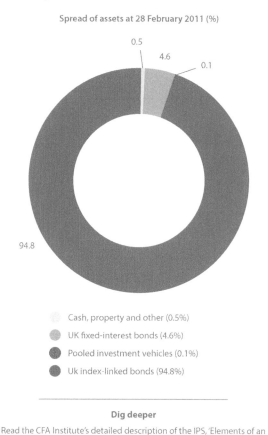

- Cash, property and other (0.5%)
- UK fixed-interest bonds (4.6%)
- Pooled investment vehicles (0.1%)
- Uk index-linked bonds (94.8%)

Dig deeper

Read the CFA Institute's detailed description of the IPS, 'Elements of an Investment Policy Statement for Institutional Investors' (www.cfainstitute. org/learning/products/publications/ccb/Pages/ccb.v2010.n13.1.aspx).

PERFORMANCE BENCHMARK

Definition: A performance benchmark is a group of assets chosen to represent the portfolio manager's investible universe and serve as a comparison point for funds and their investors.

Importance: The benchmark allows portfolio managers and investors to determine whether a fund is outperforming or underperforming the pool of assets. It is also used to measure performance consistency, relative to the benchmark, to determine risk.

It is important to select or design the right benchmark for your fund as you want to be measured against the right basket of assets. If your fund is a mixture of equity and debt, then your benchmark should also be a mixture of equity and debt.

Example: Mainstream UK funds may use the FTSE All-Share Index as a benchmark. This index contains about 750 of the largest companies listed on the UK stock exchange.

Specialised funds tend to use more specific indices to reflect the sectors in which they invest. A healthcare fund may use the S&P 500 Health Care Index while the MSCI World Financials Index could be the most appropriate for a financials fund.

RISK VERSUS REWARD

Definition: With greater risk, you have the potential for greater rewards. In simple investment terms, this means that if you invest in an asset which has the potential for high appreciation and/or high cash payments, it is likely that this investment also has a higher-than-average chance of generating negative returns or will need to be held for a longer period of time before the returns are realised.

The IPS should describe the investor's general philosophy regarding tolerance for risk. The IPS should acknowledge that the portfolio will be subject to risk and have the potential for returns to be both positive and negative over time. Relevant risks are usually myriad and may include liquidity, legal, political, regulatory, longevity, mortality and/or business risks.

In addition to specifying relevant risks, defining acceptable paths of risk in the IPS may also be important. In light of institutional risks – for example, donation activity, enrolment trends, funded status – volatility as a descriptive measure of risk may be irrelevant beyond an absolute level of loss that would completely derail an investment portfolio.

Importance: One of the greatest responsibilities of the portfolio manager is defining the fund's approach to risk and managing this risk throughout the fund's life.

Example: Institutional investors often attempt to quantify their tolerance for risk by relating returns, volatility of returns and correlation of returns of assets with a liability profile, e.g. an actuarial analysis of liabilities or specification of an eleemosynary spending policy. Much of this analysis may serve as the basis for an asset-allocation plan, and related analysis is often organised as a risk budget, the details of which need not necessarily be included in the IPS document.

Note: Risk is analysed in much greater detail in 'DIFFERENT TYPES OF RISK' on page 62.

Dig deeper

Read SEIC's Morningstar's Understanding Benchmarks (www.seic.com/doc/ invNews/documents/morningstar.pdf).

CHANGE IN BOB'S INVESTMENT STRATEGY

After many years, Bob's balanced portfolio has performed well. Bob was able to buy his new car, he was able to build an extension to his house, and he saved a decent amount for education and retirement funds.

Now Bob also decides to start up his own business. Though he is hopeful this business will do well, he has less firm an idea of his future earnings and so his top priority with his investments is to retain the wealth he has and eliminate as much risk as possible.

Bob and Samantha meet to discuss his goals and match them with various investment instruments currently available. Bob decides to divest all of his individual stocks, purchase a few equity funds, and move most of his investments into less-risky fixed-income instruments.

With Bob's greater wealth, he also has options to invest in certain funds that require a minimum investment, which are known to perform a bit better. With this change in strategy, Bob is much more comfortable knowing he doesn't have to be concerned about his current savings while he focuses on trying to grow his start-up company.

CHAPTER 7.
RISK OVERVIEW

OBJECTIVES

1. **Explain the different types of risk.**

2. **Be able to calculate volatility risk for a stock.**

DIFFERENT TYPES OF RISK

Definition: Risk describes the probability of an asset not performing as you would hope. It is the potential for an asset to lose value and for you to therefore lose money.

If you invest in a company you must consider all that could occur to cause that investment to underperform or become valueless. There is a risk the company may not execute on its strategy. There is a risk the economy enters a recession or certain changes render the company's products useless. There is a risk that the company's debt payments become too great, or a down year requires the company to file for bankruptcy because it can't make the interest payments. There is a risk the company has to delist from a major exchange and your investment in the company becomes impossible to sell. There is a risk that its returns on investments in other currencies are devalued due to exchange rates significantly dropping. There is also a risk that the country in which it operates decides to take over the company and give nothing to its shareholders. All of these risks need to be considered when making an investment as they are the foundation for determining the required rate of return used when valuing companies.

All these risks mentioned fall under the categories of business risk, market risk, financial risk, liquidity risk, exchange rate risk and country risk and are discussed in the following sections. This is not an exhaustive list but the standard risks.

Importance: Every investment comes with risk. Even when the term 'risk-free' is used in finance to describe government bonds, it is important to realise that there is even a risk that the largest government in the world could default, albeit a very small probability.

Example: Examples of risk are generally explained in terms of underperformance or as a complete loss of an investment. These are the risks that occur with investment in equities and bonds.

There are also investments that can cause extreme damage to a portfolio, where the loss can be significantly greater than the investment itself.

Dig deeper

Read the *Financial Literates* article '15 Types of Risk that affect your Investments' by Hemant Beniwal for a good overview of standard risks.

To learn about risks you probably haven't thought about before, read *Fooled by Randomness: The Hidden Role of Chance in Life and in the Markets*, by Nassim Nicholas Taleb.

VOLATILITY RISK

Definition: Volatility risk is the uncertainty of the future price of an asset or fund. The more volatile a price is, the more risk an investment will have. This risk is measured using statistics such as standard deviation, which is the fluctuation of a price, or beta, which is the fluctuation of a price relative to the market.

Importance: You need to know the level of volatility there is in the price of an asset to determine whether it fits your investment objectives. For example, if you are managing a fund where you and your clients expect consistent returns, then a volatile asset should generally be avoided.

There are cases where two volatile assets, when part of a fund, can produce consistent returns for a fund. This works when the assets are volatile, but in opposite directions at the same time.

Example: Stock A consistently returns 10% per year. Stock B generates positive returns, but much less consistently.

STOCK A	STOCK RETURN	BENCHMARK RETURN	DIFFERENCE IN RETURN
2011	10%	8%	+2%
2012	10%	14%	−4%
2013	10%	4%	+6%

STOCK B	STOCK RETURN	BENCHMARK RETURN	DIFFERENCE IN RETURN
2011	7%	8%	−1%
2012	15%	14%	+1%
2013	5%	4%	+1%

To measure the inconsistency of a stock – i.e. its volatility – it is best to use standard deviation as a measure.

STANDARD DEVIATION

Standard deviation is used to measure the consistency of a stock's returns and looks at the returns on an absolute basis, which means it doesn't consider how the market performed.

Stock A = StdDev(+10%, +10%, +10%)

Stock A = 0.00

Stock B = StdDev(+7%, +15%, +5%)

Stock B = 0.05

Stock A has lower volatility than Stock B, which means it has been a lower-risk asset and would be viewed as the better option if you are just looking at the volatility risk.

For measuring a fund's volatility, an example is available in the section 'FUND PERFORMANCE AND RANKINGS' on page 15.

BUSINESS RISK

Definition: Business risk is the uncertainty of income flow caused by the nature of a firm's business operations. Sales and revenue volatility, unanticipated fluctuations in operating costs and changes in the costs of inputs and raw materials, and the degree of operating leverage determine the level of business risk. Business risk is particularly high for start-up companies, where the business model is generally not yet proven and many assumptions are made to derive the company's projections.

Business risk is commonly determined by analysing the industry in which the company operates, the management team and its experience in the market, the company's past performance, and competitive threats.

Importance: You need to analyse the company's operations, the market, the competitors, and general business trends to determine the level of risk within a company's ability to generate a consistent, positive cash flow. In the case of excessive business risk, the individual must include an appropriate business risk-premium when determining the required rate of return.

Example: A start-up company in the biotech industry with a team of young scientists will have a significantly greater business risk than an established restaurant company that has a seasoned management team, loyal customer base and has been in operation for many years.

MARKET RISK

Definition: Market risk is the uncertainty of the macroeconomic environment, such as consumer confidence risks, interest rate risks, inflation risks, risk of a banking crisis, and so forth. Market risks are higher when an event is looming and its outcome is unknown. This may happen when a crisis in one country potentially adversely affects other countries, elections are pending and the outcome could affect regulations on an industry, or a trend in unemployment may reduce consumer confidence causing consumers to spend less, which will create even more job losses.

Market risk is usually measured by looking at trends in macroeconomic data, understanding what economists are forecasting, and examining the polling data that captures what experts predict about future economic trends.

Importance: Understanding market risk allows you to evaluate factors outside of the control of the company that could adversely affect the stock's value. A company with a high-performing management team with excellent products may still be exposed to market risks.

Example: The automotive industry serves as a good example of an industry greatly exposed to market risks. A car company may develop a line of automobiles that people think are fantastic and the management team may be the best in the industry, but if unemployment is high, inflation is high, and consumer confidence is low, it will have a very difficult time selling cars, no matter how good they are.

FINANCIAL RISK

Definition: Financial risk is the uncertainty caused by the use of debt-financing. Borrowing requires fixed payments which must be paid ahead of payments to stockholders.

Financial risk is often measured using key financial ratios, such as total debt/total assets and earnings before interest and taxes (EBIT)/interest expenses. There are also rating agencies that estimate the risk of a company defaulting on its debt and assign various ratings to the bonds themselves. The ones that are rated the riskiest are often termed 'junk bonds'.

Importance: As a shareholder, the greater the amount of debt a company has outstanding, the greater amount of interest the company must pay to its debtholders. This means there is a greater risk that the stockholders won't receive as much in the form of net income if other risks affect the performance of the company. There is also a greater chance that the company will be forced into bankruptcy if it is unable to make the interest payments to its debtholders, which could result in the shares being valueless.

For bondholders, the greater the financial risk, the higher the probability that the company will default on its debt obligations, thus the coupon payments will stop and the bond's value will be greatly reduced, if not deemed valueless.

Example: Companies that invest heavily in their own infrastructure generally experience the greatest financial risk. For example, consider the decision to invest in A-Mart or B-Mart, large retail stores that sell similar products in similar regions. A-Mart owns all of its stores and borrows quite heavily to do so, while B-Mart leases its stores. A portfolio manager must factor A-Mart's increased financial risk into an investment decision.

CORRUPTION AND INTEGRITY RISK

Definition: Corruption and integrity risk is the uncertainty of whether the people involved in a company you are investing in or are doing business with are involved in illegal and unethical business practices.

Importance: When investing with an individual, in a fund or in a company, it is incredibly important to do a background check. When invested, you must monitor performance and question suspicious activities. When behaviour seems suspicious, it is best not to invest, as corruption and integrity risk is one of the most dangerous – it could wipe out the complete value of your investment.

Example: There are several examples of fund managers stealing from their investors with Ponzi schemes and executives stealing or redirecting money from public companies. Bernard Madoff is one of the most famous instances of the former. He stole billions of dollars from his investors. Kenneth Lay and Jeffrey Skilling are some of the most famous examples of the latter. They redirected funds into personal businesses, sold significant shares prior to their company's collapse, and held elaborate parties for themselves and family members at the company's expense.

LIQUIDITY RISK

Definition: Liquidity risk is the uncertainty of being able to sell your investment, of how long it might take should you be able to do so, and whether the valuation will be fair.

Liquidity risk varies by asset type. For example, it is common knowledge that publicly-traded stocks are far more liquid than real estate or private equity in a company. With that said, there is the risk that certain asset types will fall out of favour and go from being very liquid to being completely illiquid, meaning nobody will purchase them.

BOB: A HIGHLY DESIRED CLIENT

Bob's business turns out to be a great success and Bob not only grows it into a larger company, he ends up taking the company public and it is eventually bought out by a larger public company. Bob now has more money than he knows what to do with and as such has lots of people who want to invest his money for him.

Bob decides to move to Florida. He buys a house in an exclusive country club community and starts playing golf. One day on the golf course, a fellow golfer mentions that he has been making a lot of money from an investment fund his fund manager friend selected for him. His fund manager friend has asked to meet Bob. The golfer tells Bob this investor is amazing; when the markets go up his fund goes up, when the markets go down, his fund still goes up. In fact, the golfer brags that he is able to live off of the dividends paid by the fund and the value of his investment held by the fund still increases. Bob is very interested: not only would he be able to maintain his lifestyle, he would also be able to leave a nice inheritance to his children and grandchildren.

Bob meets with the golfer's friend to better understand the opportunity. After a few meetings with the head of the fund, Bob feels he has a good grasp of how the investments are managed, and he is impressed with its performance and the number of celebrities invested in it.

Before Bob sends any money to the fund manager, he calls Samantha. Samantha warns Bob that if it sounds too good to be true, it probably is. There have been many people who have exaggerated their performance and taken advantage of people who are not as knowledgeable about investing, naturally trusting, and want to believe they can gain returns well above the market's performance every year.

Bob decides to take his broker's advice and not invest in this fund. As it turns out, it ends up being a Ponzi scheme just like the ones Bernie Madoff and many others have set up in the past.

A Ponzi scheme works in the following way. Firstly, it falsifies its fund value and performance to show above-market returns. This performance attracts more investors, and more investors mean the fund continually gets more money to pay out dividends to existing investors. As long as people keep receiving their dividend cheque and statements showing their investments are increasing better than the market, they will keep their investments with the fund.

Ponzi schemes are usually exposed when the fund runs out of money. When an investor doesn't receive his dividend payment, he becomes suspicious and requests the balance of his portfolio be sent to him, at which time it becomes clear there is no money left. This is particularly tragic when someone is retired, dependent upon the dividend payments to live, and has trusted a dishonest person with all of his savings.

Judging liquidity risk also requires the investor to look at the individual assets within an asset class. With stocks, liquidity is measured by looking at a company's outstanding shares not held by insiders (free float) compared with its total shares outstanding – as well as the amount of shares that trade on average per day (average trading volume).

If a company's free float percentage is low and very few shares trade per day, you can be fairly certain that if you are purchasing a large amount of shares your order will drive the price up. Likewise, if you are selling those shares back into the same market, you will be driving the price down, which means you will be buying higher and selling lower than what the market price was stated at prior to you placing your order.

Importance: When evaluating an investment, you need to understand that there is a risk the asset you are acquiring may fall out of favour and it may be difficult to sell that asset when you want to liquidate your holding.

Example: In 2009, many funds were investing in real-estate derivatives, which seemed like a good investment due to the ever-increasing price of these assets and the liquid market for these instruments. But as investors came to realise that they knew very little about the underlying assets linked to these derivatives, the market for them stopped working – many investors wanted to sell the assets, but no investor wanted to purchase them. This market became completely illiquid and because of that, the market value of those assets fell close to zero.

EXCHANGE-RATE RISK

Definition: Exchange-rate risk is the uncertainty of returns on investments that are held in a different currency than your own. Changes in exchange rates affect your return when converting an investment back into your home currency.

Exchange rates move based on expected inflation between and among the countries and the geopolitical regions that share a currency (such as the euro), but since there are many factors that influence inflation, such as the health of a country's economy, lots of these factors are analysed and will have an effect on the movement of exchange rates.

Importance: It is easy to lose sight of exchange-rate risk when considering investments in other established countries as you might assume the rates don't change considerably. But if rates have fluctuated considerably from year to year, then returns on an investment in a company that performs well in a strong market could be discounted by the impact of an exchange rate that doesn't move in your favour.

Example: The previous chart depicts the relation of the British pound to the US dollar over a five-year period. If you just consider the change in the exchange rate over the past three years, you would feel comfortable that your investment in the other country has a low risk of being adversely affected by changes in the exchange rate. But, looking at 2008 and 2009, there was a significant change in the exchange rate: an investment in early 2008 would have lost 25% of its value by the beginning of 2009.

COUNTRY RISK

Definition: Country risk is associated with the political risk and uncertainty of returns caused by the possibility of a major change in the political or economic environment in a country.

Importance: Individuals who invest in countries that have unstable political and economic systems must include a country risk premium when determining their required rate of return.

Example: The next figure shows an overview of the mean country risk as calculated by *Euromoney*. An investment in the darker-shaded countries involves less country risk than those in the lighter-shaded countries.

The absolute numbers are important as well as the trends. The second figure shows the direction in which the countries are moving based on *Euromoney*'s data. Even though a country has low risk in terms of its political government, if the country is becoming less stable overall, an investment in that country will become riskier.

Mean Country Risk, March 2000 - March 2011, Euromoney data

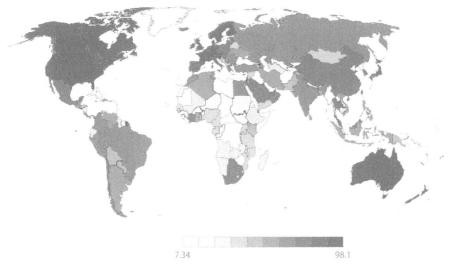

7.34   98.1

Annual Trend in Country Risk, March 2000 - March 2011, Euromoney data

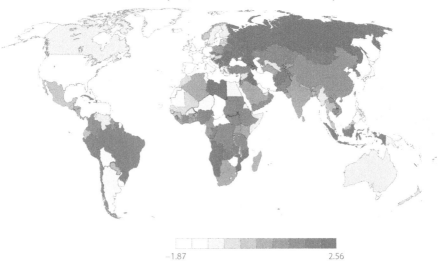

−1.87   2.56

Source: Data taken from country risk data in *Euromoney* magazine. Chart was created using the "worldmap" package in R v. 2.13.0, and rendered using the "Cairo" package

CHAPTER 8.
INVESTMENT PHILOSOPHIES

OBJECTIVES

1. Understand the importance of defining a fund's investment philosophies.

2. Decide which philosophies work best for your fund.

3. Grasp the core analysis required for each investment philosophy.

INVESTMENT PHILOSOPHY

Definition: An investment philosophy is a set of rules, behaviours and procedures designed to guide a portfolio manager's selection of an investment portfolio.

Common investment philosophies include value, growth, and growth at a reasonable price (GARP) investing. There isn't a correct investment philosophy and portfolio managers will often incorporate several of them into their investment process.

Importance: Defining a fund's investment philosophy is important for directing the analysis and criteria that will be used to select assets for the fund's portfolio. A consistent approach assists with the decision-making process.

Your philosophy will be affected by your experiences in the markets and how they work; they will evolve over time and your investment strategies will need to change as well.

Example: The following is Cornerstone's investment philosophy as published on its website:

> *The basis for Cornerstone's philosophy is that investors overreact in the short run due to emotional stress or excessive optimism. As a result, the market constantly mis-prices securities relative to their long-term value.*

VALUE INVESTING

Definition: Value investing involves identifying and investing in stocks that appear to be undervalued.

To determine whether a company is undervalued, the portfolio manager needs to value the company or compare the company's valuation multiples, such as P/E ratios, relative to the company's peers. Benjamin Graham is often referred to as the founder of this philosophy and Warren Buffett credits him with providing the basis of his investment philosophy.

Value investing is like looking for a cheap house in an expensive neighbourhood. The theory is that, with time, the house's value will increase at a greater rate than the value of the other houses in the neighbourhood.

Importance: Value investing has been around for many years and is a common philosophy adopted by funds and investors. It is common because it is easy to understand, and the criteria used are easy to monitor.

In the chart that follows, the performance of the iShares S&P Value Index compared with the S&P 500 over two years shows that the two indices traded similarly for the first six months and the last six months – but the value index underperformed the market for the middle 12 months. This implies that the market was largely focused on value investing during the first and last six months, and during the middle 12 months adopted slightly different philosophies.

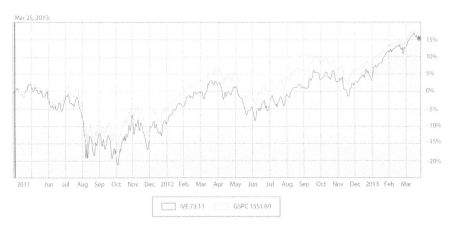

Example: Examples of some screening criteria used by value and growth investors, most of which have been promoted by Ben Graham himself:

- **Price to earnings (P/E) ratio of the stock has less than 40% of the average P/E over the last five years.** The P/E ratio is used to compare a company's market value (price per share) to the company's earnings (earnings per share). If the company's current P/E ratio is high compared to its historical P/E ratio, then it might be viewed as overvalued.

- **Dividend yield > two thirds of the Treasury bond yield.** The dividend yield is the annual dividend a company pays divided by the current price of the company's stock. The dividend yield is an indicator of the cash return you will receive from owning the stock. If your return is close to what you will receive from risk-free investments and you have the potential upside of the increase in the stock price, the stock might be undervalued.

- **Price is less than two thirds of the book value per share.** The book value per share is the value of a company's assets that are attributed to the equity holders. Another way to think about this is if you take all of the assets the company owns and subtract the value of the liabilities the company has, the remaining value of assets is what is available for the people that own the company's stock. If you divide this value by the shares outstanding, then you will have the book value per share. If the price per share is less than the value of the assets available to the shareholders (book value per share), then the stock might be undervalued.

- **Historical earnings per share (EPS) growth over last 10 years > 7%.** EPS is used to determine the portion of a company's net income attributed to one share of the company's stock. If this is growing by 7% per annum, it can be expected that the company's stock price will be increasing at a similar rate. This screen will give you a good indication of whether a company is a growth company.

GROWTH INVESTING

Definition: Growth investing involves identifying and investing in companies that consistently experience above-average increases in sales and earnings.

To determine whether the increases are above average, the portfolio manager compares the growth rates of a company's revenue and earnings to its peers.

Growth investing is like supporting sports teams that have winning records. Instead of being loyal to your local team, you switch your support throughout the year to the teams that are doing the best or recruiting the best talent in the expectation that your chances of having a team win the league will be significantly better.

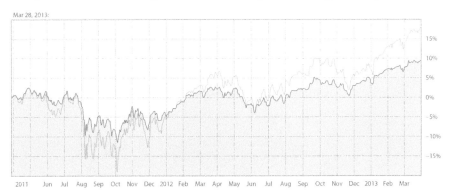

Importance: Growth investing is another of the most common philosophies adopted by funds and investors. The criteria is simple to monitor and investors can simultaneously employ their own purchasing experiences in this strategy by investing in companies where they see themselves and friends purchasing more of a company's product.

The chart on the previous page compares the performance of the iShares S&P Growth Allocation index to the S&P 500 index over two years, and shows that the two indices traded similarly for the first year but the growth index underperformed the market for most of the second year. This implies that the market was largely focused on growth investing during the first year and adopted slightly different philosophies during the second.

Example: Following are some screen criteria used by growth investors:

- P/E < expected growth rate (same as price/earnings to growth [PEG] < 1)
- low PEG ratio stocks (PEG ratio = P/E ÷ long-term expected growth)
- earnings expected to grow at an increasing rate in the next two years
- small cap investing, as small companies are expected to grow at a faster rate than large companies.

GARP INVESTING

Definition: GARP is the hybrid of value investing and growth investing.

This philosophy asserts that you can't look at growth without considering value. A company that fits with GARP philosophy needs to meet growth investing criteria as well as value investing criteria.

Importance: Warren Buffett once said that "growth and value are joined at the hip". GARP investing focuses on both the growth and value traits of a stock to derive a more balanced approach. There are several companies that can be viewed as both value and growth and this investment philosophy focuses on that universe.

Example: The screening criteria used for GARP investing is a combination of the criteria listed in value and growth. The common screening criteria used by GARP investors are:

- low PEG ratio stocks (PEG ratio = PE ÷ long-term expected growth) relative to their peers

- P/E ratio greater than 0, but less than 20 [or any number that makes most sense to the industry].

GLOBAL MACRO INVESTING

Definition: Global macro investing is a cross-asset philosophy focusing on a holistic economic perspective, taking expected changes of gross domestic product (GDP), political events and views of various countries into account. The philosophy asserts that if the people who live in a country are increasing their production and making more money, the value of companies in that country will increase in value. This includes the equity, debt and derivatives that are linked to these companies as well as the bonds associated with the country.

Importance: Global macro investing is well-known and is implemented when selecting investments due to country risk as well as exchange-rate risk, but it is not used as widely as a stand-alone strategy.

Some major investors, such as George Soros, have used this as an exclusive strategy. It is a more volatile mode of investing, since predicting what will happen within a country is much more difficult than predicting what will happen within a company. Simply put, these strategies tend to be more complex, investments tend to be more volatile, generally resulting in very large gains or losses.

Example: Global macro investing is made up of many different strategies as investors look across country performance, e.g. GDP, unemployment, government policy (taxes, regulations), monetary factors (inflation), exchange rates, as well as many others.

LEO: INVESTMENT STRATEGY

Leo considers himself a value investor. He has set up stock screens that focus on valuation multiples, such as price/earnings or dividend yield, to help him evaluate his portfolio and determine where he should be investing. These screens identify companies that appear to be undervalued relative to peer companies. Leo invests in the undervalued companies until the price rises to the point where they no longer appear undervalued. Sometimes a price doesn't rise like Leo hoped for and instead a company's earnings decrease, which will also affect the valuation multiple. So, Leo needs to make sure a company that appears to be undervalued is actually undervalued and isn't priced lower than its peers because its future financials won't be as strong.

Even though Leo is focused on value investing, he does make changes to his portfolio based on how he sees the market valuing stocks. As such, he continuously analyses the performance of the companies within his investible universe to try and determine how other investors in the market are investing. If there is a greater focus on buying and selling on the basis of events in the news, Leo will set aside a portion of his portfolio for speculative investing.

Leo is careful not to commit too much of his time or his assets under management in his portfolio to this strategy as he doesn't want to appear to be changing his investment philosophy. He has stated to those that invest in his fund that he is a value investor, and he doesn't wish to appear dishonest.

EVENT-DRIVEN INVESTING

Definition: Event-driven investing is a philosophy of investing in assets based on expected or announced corporate events. These events are generally corporate actions such as mergers, acquisitions, spin-offs and bankruptcies.

The portfolio managers who adopt this philosophy focus on identifying potential events with the goal of exploiting inefficiencies (arbitrage opportunities) in the market.

Importance: Event-driven investing requires carefully-thought-out investment strategies on how to react to the announcement of various events. Not only does a fund manager need to have a good source for learning about these events, he needs to be able to react quickly in order to maximise his return on investment.

Example: One example of executing on the occurrence of an event is the announcement of an acquisition:

Company A announces the acquisition of B Corporation

These deals are generally announced while the markets for both Company A and B are closed. Therefore, a fund manager needs to very quickly evaluate the terms of the transaction and decide how he will invest. The acquisition price for B Corporation will generally include a significant premium.

As the announcement occurs while the market is closed, the price of the target will generally open close to the acquisition price, but this price is often still below what the acquiring company is offering as there is a risk the deal won't close, for various reasons, and the completion of deals generally takes several months.

The event-driven fund manager needs to evaluate the transaction and determine whether he will purchase the target company's shares, short the acquiring company's shares, or both.

SPECULATIVE INVESTING

Definition: Speculative investing is a philosophy of investing in companies where there isn't a great deal of knowledge about the underlying performance or valuation of the asset, but there is a feeling that the price will rise.

The feeling can be based on what the portfolio manager has 'heard on the street', past price performance ('the price keeps going up, so it must be a good investment'), or unique insight about the price performance. Speculative investing is often the reason for pricing bubbles in certain assets.

Importance: Speculative investing is as much behavioural as it is about having a source of unique knowledge about the price performance of an asset. This doesn't make it a bad philosophy, but the risks and rewards are often greater with speculative investing.

Example: Some examples of speculative investing are real estate and gold.

The US real estate market, represented by the iShares Dow Jones US Real Estate index, generated very good returns from 2003 to 2007. The high returns attracted speculative investors, which generated a bubble in real estate values. When the market reacted to the overvaluations, the prices dropped significantly. From the peak to the trough, within one year, the value dropped by approximately 70%. Since the correction, prices have regained a significant portion of their pre-bust value.

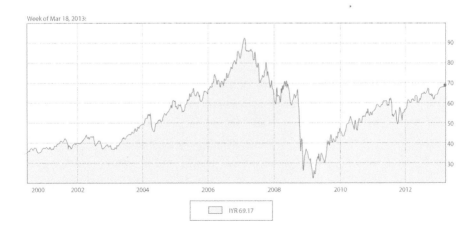

Week of Mar 18, 2013:

IYR 69.17

Gold may be viewed as another speculative investment as the price performance is based on a perceived value of the metal and not the demand for the commodity within the production of any product.

The price of gold has been based on how nervous investors are investing in other assets, such as equity or bonds. More investors invest in gold, increasing its price and attracting even more speculative investors. It may be another bubble or the current price may be sustainable based on the uncertainty in other financial markets.

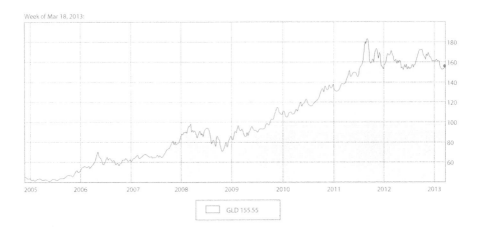

Week of Mar 18, 2013:

GLD 155.55

BOB: IRRATIONAL EXUBERANCE

Now that Bob doesn't have to work, is getting sick of golf, and has a great deal of money to invest, his mind is starting to wander and he's looking for new opportunities that will keep him occupied as well as increase his wealth. One of Bob's old business partners tells him about an emerging technology industry that will change the way companies do business.

In fact, Bob's old partner is such a strong believer in this emerging industry that he has invested his complete savings as well as additional borrowed money to maximise his return. His investments have so far paid off – stock prices in this industry have increased by over 200% in the past year.

After narrowly avoiding investing his hard-earned money in a Ponzi scheme, Bob has become much more careful about whose investing advice he takes. Bob decides to phone Samantha, his most trusted advisor. Samantha is very aware of the outstanding performance of this industry, but doesn't quite understand what these companies do or why they have such high valuations; they don't seem to be profitable.

Samantha asks Bob for help to understand what these companies do and when they will become profitable. As Bob doesn't know, he sets up a meeting with his old business partner to discuss. Bob asks him to explain what exactly these companies do, why it will change the world of business, what evidence he has to show this change will materialise, and when these companies will be profitable.

Slightly offended, and perhaps a little embarrassed, Bob's old business partner tries to explain the industry and answer the rest of the questions, but ends by saying, "Look, there are far smarter people than me that can answer these questions and are invested in these companies. Just look at their performance – you can tell this is a good investment."

Bob takes his notes back to Samantha and tries to explain these scant details to her. At this point, she recommends he reads the book *Irrational Exuberance* by Robert J. Shiller, as it explains more of the behavioural aspects of the market and may help him understand what is really driving prices here.

One of the quotes from the book that sticks with Bob is the observation that: *"[p]eople still place too much confidence in the markets and have too strong a belief that paying attention to the gyrations in their investments will someday make them rich, and so they do not make conservative preparations for possible bad outcomes."* As Bob doesn't really understand the emerging industry his friend has told him about, and would be placing too much confidence in only what the market was telling him (the price increase), he decides not to invest.

As it turns out, the market for the emerging industry Bob was looking at soon crashes. Stock prices collapse to a fraction of their peak when investors start to question whether the emerging industry's business models are truly grounded in reality. It emerges that many investors had assumed there was value there only because of the continual price rises.

In the crash of 2008, when investors started to question the value of real estate and derivatives that were difficult to understand, the whole market started selling to the point where nobody remained a buyer. Warren Buffett described them as "time bombs" and "financial weapons of mass destruction". When there was nobody left to purchase them, values dropped to zero and some markets froze. Fortunately for Bob's old business partner, there are still some buyers as he begins to sell his holdings, but he loses all of his gains and walks away with far less than he originally invested. Soon he is forced to come out of retirement in order to replenish his savings.

DESIGNING, BUILDING AND MANAGING A PORTFOLIO

4

However beautiful the strategy, you should occasionally look at the results.

Winston Churchill

CHAPTER 9.
FRAMEWORK AND ASSET ALLOCATION

OBJECTIVES

1. Learn the principles of designing a portfolio and the importance of tracking your decision-making process.

2. Understand how to design a portfolio that incorporates your investment objectives, investment philosophy and investible universe.

3. Define your asset-allocation preferences on the basis of the theories that best apply to your management style.

PORTFOLIO MANAGEMENT FRAMEWORK

Definition: Designing your portfolio is the process of combining your investment objectives, investment philosophies and investible universe into a finite number of investments, weighted appropriately.

The process of crafting an optimal portfolio can be incredibly complex and perhaps overwhelming. It is best to take the process one step at a time and to avoid trying to figure out the whole market before you invest. Figure out a portion of the market that best fits your investment objectives and investment philosophies before later expanding into other areas.

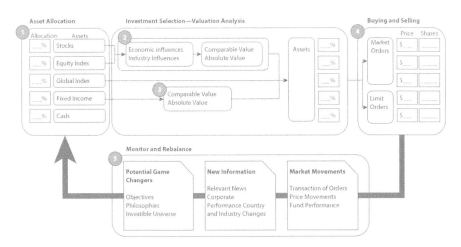

In this chapter, you will start creating your portfolio. This is not the definitive process for managing a portfolio, but it will cover the essentials. You can evolve the design as you become more comfortable with the management of your portfolio.

ASSET ALLOCATION

Define your high-level asset allocation among asset classes that best fit your objectives and philosophies. At this stage, you define which percentage of your fund you want to invest in different asset types.

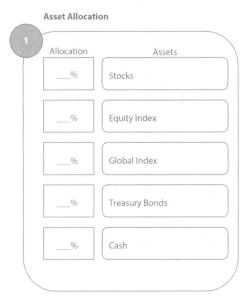

INVESTMENT SELECTION

Once you define your high-level allocation, you need to select the investments within the asset classes that best fit your objectives and philosophies.

The evaluation of stocks and equity indices is different from the evaluation of treasury bonds.

After selecting the investments, you need to decide how much of each asset to purchase. This decision will be based on your evaluations combined with your objectives and philosophies.

Investment Selection - Valuation Analysis

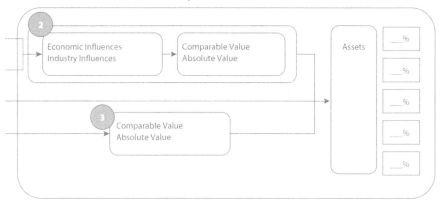

BUYING AND SELLING

After you have selected your assets and weightings, you need to buy and sell assets to get to your optimal portfolio. The transactions can be completed using both market and limit orders.

Buying and Selling

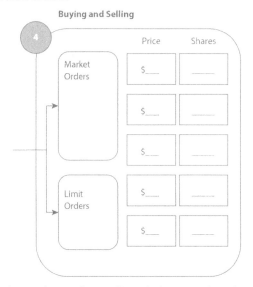

It is important to know that orders will rarely be completed at estimated prices quoted.[1] Supply and demand within the market will continually affect prices, as will news and events.

MONITOR AND REBALANCE

Monitoring changes in the market, the performance of your fund, fundamental changes of the assets within your portfolio, financial performance of companies, and events in the economy is incredibly important.

---

[1] This sentence primarily refers to orders place in a Market-Class simulation.

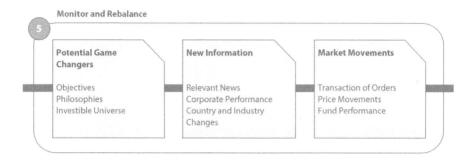

The information gained from monitoring – combined with reflection on investment objectives, investment philosophy and the investible universe – allows a fund manager to optimally rebalance a fund's portfolio.

Importance: How you design your portfolio is incredibly important, but what is truly vital is not the end result of the design as much as it is the decision-making process that goes into the design. You should track why you make the decisions you do, as it is likely your objectives or philosophies will change over time. It's likely that the assumptions you make about certain asset classes or investments will not hold true in the future. So you'll want to revisit your portfolio design decisions periodically and record your design principles to evaluate and test your assumptions further on.

ASSET ALLOCATION

Definition: Asset allocation is the decision that the fund manager makes on the percentage of asset types in which he will invest. These decisions should be purely based on the fund's investment objectives.

The core factors the portfolio manager must consider are: (a) how much cash the fund will need to disperse in the future and when; (b) which benchmark the fund's performance will be compared with; and (c) how risk averse the fund needs to be for its investor base.

With these considerations, the portfolio manager will be able to select the type of assets that are most appropriate for the fund and how much of each asset type the fund should hold at any period of time.

Importance: Selecting the appropriate asset allocation is a critical feature for defining a fund's portfolio, as this will have a significant effect on your fund's performance. Ibbotson Associates' study, 'Does Asset Allocation Policy Explain 40, 90, or 100 Percent of Performance?', concludes that asset-allocation decisions determine about 100% of investment performance for those who follow a low-cost, long-term investing strategy. This doesn't mean that the asset-allocation decision is the only decision to make, but it does play a major role in your fund's performance.

Example: If stocks decreased by 20% last year and bonds grew by 10%, funds with different asset allocations would perform differently. Based on the allocations in the example below:

	FUND A	FUND B	FUND C
Bonds	80%	50%	20%
Stocks	20%	50%	80%
Performance	+4%	−5%	−14%

Fund A outperformed Fund B by 9% and Fund C by 18%.

SIMPLE ASSET ALLOCATION

Definition: A simple way to decide on the asset allocation that works for your fund is by using your investment objectives as the foundation and deciding on how risky you want to design your portfolio to be. The asset-allocation decision is deciding between risk and return. An investment that is low risk will have a low return and an investment with a high return will also have a high degree of risk.

If it is more important to retain wealth than grow it rapidly at a risk of losing value, then you will allocate more of your assets toward those assets that are less risky, such as bonds.

Importance: Using a simple asset-allocation model can be close to optimal, allowing a new portfolio manager to start managing a fund. There are many different models that can help you determine the optimal asset-allocation mix, but when you are new to designing a portfolio it is better to apply common sense than mathematical equations. Ultimately, the mathematical equations will provide better insight, but that can wait until you are more comfortable with managing your portfolio.

Example: Here are a few simple examples of asset-allocation decisions that can get you started with the design of your portfolio.

Fundadvice Ultimate Buy and Hold

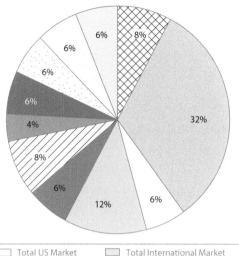

☐ Total US Market		☐ Total International Market	
■ Emerging		⧄ European	
■ Pacific		■ Large Value	
☐ Small Value		☐ Small Blend	
☐ REIT		⊠ Inflation Protected Bonds	
▨ Treasuries			

Dr. Bernstein's Smart Money

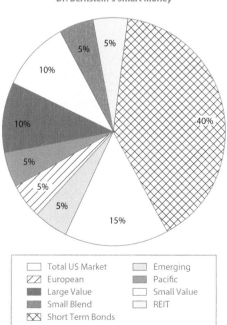

☐ Total US Market		☐ Emerging	
⧄ European		■ Pacific	
■ Large Value		☐ Small Value	
▨ Small Blend		☐ REIT	
⊠ Short Term Bonds			

Second Grader's Starter

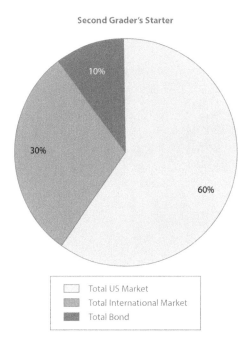

As you learn more about asset-allocation theories and become more sophisticated, you may want to employ different models in the high-level asset-allocation decision-making process.

ADVANCED-ALLOCATION MODELS

Definition: The asset-allocation decision is the decision between risk and return. Both the risk and return can be estimated by evaluating past performance of asset classes, a model that has been developed to determine the optimal asset-allocation model.

Importance: Modern portfolio theory defines how to maximise a fund's return while minimising its risk. This theory has changed the way portfolio management is analysed, by providing a mathematical understanding of the markets. However, it is not always applicable to smaller illiquid markets.

Example: Here is the 'Efficient Frontier', published by Harry Markowitz and the basis of modern portfolio theory:

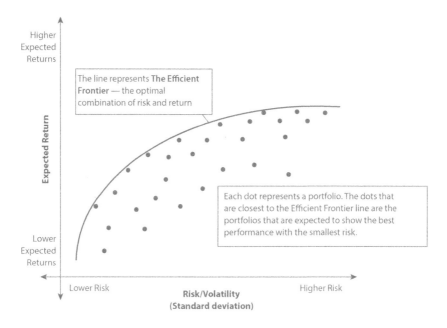

Source: smart401k.com

CHAPTER 10.
EQUITY SELECTION

OBJECTIVES

1. **Understand the principles behind selecting equities based on your investment philosophies.**

2. **Learn about the core valuation methodologies for stocks.**

3. **Learn to compare companies based on stock price and financial performance.**

4. **Calculate a company's value using the dividend discount model (DDM) and discounted cash flow (DCF) analysis.**

EQUITY-SELECTION PROCESS

Definition: The equity-selection process is designed to evaluate different economies and industries, before selecting the indices and stocks you would like to invest in.

The process presented here can be described as a top-down approach, since it starts with a high-level view and works down to individual assets. You will incorporate your investment objectives and investment philosophies when selecting which economies and industries are most appealing before ultimately selecting an index or stock.

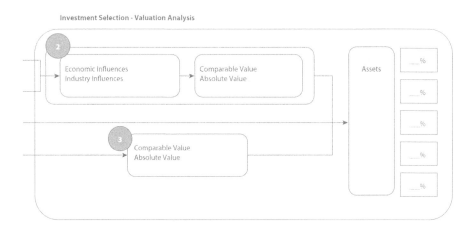

In the previous chapter, you decided which percentage of your portfolio would be allocated in equity indices and stocks. This section should help you decide which particular indices and stocks to select.

Importance: The selection of the individual assets for your portfolio will determine whether you meet your objectives, specifically whether you outperform or underperform your goals and benchmarks.

Example: Here is the top-down equity-selection process used by Bowen, Hanes and Company.

The analysis starts with a very high-level view and is very similar to the process defined within this book.

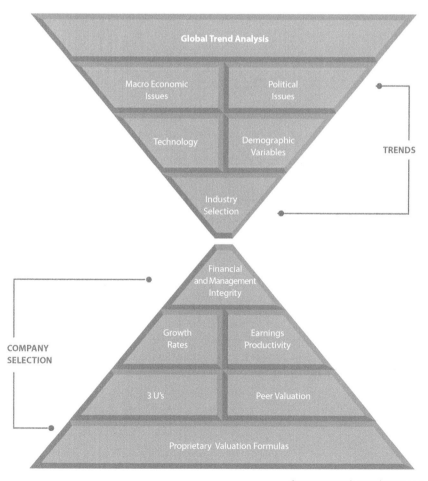

Source: www.bowenhanes.com

91

TOP-DOWN ANALYSIS

Definition: Top-down analysis is the process of starting with global and country analysis to identify how you want to weight your regional investments. For example, if you are more interested in less risk, you may find the G7 countries most attractive. Within the G7, your analysis may lead to greater investment in two countries, such as Germany and the USA, with lesser investment in the other five countries.

After selecting countries, you then need to analyse industries to determine which are the most attractive. It may be that the auto industry is most attractive in Germany and the technology sector is most attractive in the USA.

The third stage is the selection of the individual investments, whether an index, an industry, country, region or an individual stock.

Importance: A top-down analysis is designed to optimise returns by applying a high-level view of countries and industries that look best from an investment perspective. This is in contrast to narrowly focusing on a company's valuation relative to its price or screening on a company's historical stock price performance or any other factors. Top-down analysis will narrow the investment focus to a country, region, industry, or any other macro-level focus selected by the fund manager.

Example: Here is a typical top-down analysis for equity selection, moving from the geopolitical level, to industries and down to individual companies.

EXAMPLE: EQUITY SELECTION BY TOP-DOWN ANALYSIS

GEOPOLITICAL ANALYSIS

In this top-down analysis, we will use economic indicators and financial metrics to analyse the countries or regions that fit your investment objectives and philosophies best. There are many other factors you can analyse, such as monetary and fiscal policy measures, but for this analysis we will start with the basics.

Economic indicators. Economic conditions influence all industries and companies and should be analysed before making investment decisions. You need to understand where countries or regions are within their growth cycles, assuming that the economies expand and contract in discernible periods, economic indicators provide some insight into the country's business cycle, and there hasn't been a significant change to a country which renders economic indicators useless.

There are four categories of cyclical indicator that are traditionally used in assessing where economies are in their growth cycles:

- Leading indicators – economic series that usually reach peaks or troughs before corresponding peaks or troughs in aggregate economy activity. Unemployment rates are a good example of leading indicators, as businesses will start laying off employees prior to reporting disappointing numbers.

- Coincident indicators – economic series that have peaks and troughs that roughly coincide with the peaks and troughs in the business cycle.

- Lagging indicators – economic series that experience their peaks and troughs after those of the aggregate economy.

- Selected series – economic series that do not fall into one of the three main groups, such as environmental or social factors, but are important and may be relevant in the long term.

Financial Metrics. A company's performance and expected performance must be analysed, ideally aggregating the financial figures from companies operating in the selected countries.

Key financial indicators for comparison include:

1. valuation multiples and

2. growth metrics.

These are the key financial indicators to compare among all three levels. The difference lies in how the numbers are aggregated or, for individual companies, not aggregated for company analysis.

For this analysis, the financial metrics are aggregated by a company or region, to calculate the metric for the whole country. For example, we can calculate a country's price-to-earnings (P/E) ratio by adding together the market capitalisations of all of the companies in the country and dividing it by the aggregate net income for all of the companies in the country.

1. Valuation multiples – these multiples compare the value of all of the companies headquartered in the country relative to the aggregate financial performance of these companies. Some common aggregate multiples are: price to earnings (P/E), which provides insight into how the stock market values the companies in that country relative to earnings; dividend yield, which lets you know the amount of return you can expect from dividends relative to current stock prices; market capitalisation to revenue, which is similar to the P/E ratio, but looks at the value compared to the companies' revenues instead of net income; enterprise value/operating income, which provides insight into the

value of companies' equity and debt compared to the earnings made prior to paying interest and taxes.

2. Growth metrics – these metrics provide insight into historical and projected growth within a country. The most common growth metrics are revenue, operating income, and net income. Using estimate data from equity research analysts, it is also common to use an aggregated estimated long-term growth and price targets.

Using these economic indicators and financial metrics, you can compare countries, analyse historical trends, and identify which countries are most attractive for your investment objectives and philosophies. This analysis provides insight into which countries are most attractive from a country index and stock perspective.

INDUSTRY ANALYSIS

In this second stage of the top-down analysis, we consider the prospects of industries within an economy. At any given time, some industries grow while others fail, some industries depend upon others due to relationships based on the supply chain of a product or service, some industries thrive when the economy is stagnant or falls, some industries experience significant structural or regulatory changes.

In industry analysis, you need to look at many influences that could affect an industry. Within our analysis, we will focus on economic influences, operating changes, life cycle and financial metrics.

There are other factors that will affect industries, such as country demographics, lifestyles, technology, politics and regulations, but we are going to focus on the core drivers.

Economic influences. Economic variables to monitor are inflation, interest rates, international economic and consumer sentiment. You need to know how these indicators affect the industries as they may impact different industries differently.

Economic trends can and do affect industry performance. By identifying and monitoring key assumptions and variables, you can monitor the economy and gauge the implications of new information in your industry analysis.

Operating changes. Industries are constantly changing and you must determine whether the changes are cyclical in nature or due to structural changes.

Cyclical changes in an economy arise from the ups and downs of the business cycle. These changes can be identified by comparing an industry's operating metrics, such as revenue growth, or valuation multiples such as P/E, to historical trends within the industry. If it appears the industry is growing or contracting due to cyclical economic events, then you can include this in your analysis. If leading indicators show the industry traditionally grows when certain events occur, then the industry will be an attractive investment.

Structural changes occur when an economy undergoes a major change in organisation or how it functions. Some describe the industry after a structural change as 'the new normal', implying that all assumptions made based on past performance cannot be used in the new environment.

The music industry is a good example of this. Structural changes due to the distribution, consumption and sharing of music over the internet fundamentally altered how the industry operates and profits from music.

Life cycle. Most sectors or industries are characterised by a five-stage life cycle: development, rapid growth, mature growth, stabilisation and decline. Industries at the beginning and end of their life cycle are riskier investments, but can also provide significant returns.

Each of these stages raises different questions you want to ask and explore. The basics include identifying the competitive characteristics of an industry: is it competitive, heavily regulated, monopolistic? What are the barriers to new entrants? What could significantly disrupt how companies operate?

Financial metrics. Companies' performance and expected performance within industries needs analysis. In doing this, it's ideal to aggregate the financial figures from the industries that operate in countries selected by our geopolitical analysis.

This is a repeat of the geopolitical analysis, but it is important to keep consistency within this section. The key financial indicators to compare are valuation multiples and growth metrics. These are the key financial indicators to compare on all three levels. The difference is how the numbers are aggregated, or for individual companies, not aggregated for the company analysis.

For this analysis, the financial metrics are aggregated on a company or regional level to calculate the metric for the whole country. For example, we can calculate a country's P/E ratio by adding together the market capitalisations of all of the companies in the country and dividing it by the aggregate net income for all of the companies in the country.

Valuation multiples – these multiples compare the way the industry is valued relative to its financial performance. The most common multiples are P/E, dividend yield, market capitalisation/revenue, enterprise value/ operating income (EBIT or EBITDA), and enterprise value/revenue.

Growth metrics – these metrics provide insight into the historical and projected growth within an industry. The most common growth metrics are revenue, operating income and net income. Using estimates from equity research analysts, it is also common to use aggregated estimated long-term growth and price targets.

Analysing these economic influences, operating changes, life cycle and financial metrics we can compare industries, analyse historical trends and identify which industries are most attractive to our investment objectives and philosophies. This analysis provides insight into which industries are most attractive from an industry index and stock perspective.

COMPANY ANALYSIS

The analysis of companies and their stocks is the final step in the top-down approach of investing. Companies can be evaluated using the methods explained in the following sections within this book: 'COMPARABLE COMPANY ANALYSIS' on page 100, 'DIVIDEND-DISCOUNT MODEL' on page 103 and 'DISCOUNTED CASH FLOW' on page 105. You need to refer to these sections to make a valuation decision on which companies to include in your portfolio.

We are also interested in the 'softer' strategic aspects: strengths, weaknesses, opportunities and threats (SWOT) analysis and competitive position. You must consider a company's current rivalries in its industry: the threat of new entrants, potential substitute products, the bargaining power of suppliers, and the bargaining power of buyers, to name but a few factors.

Is the company's strategy appropriate? Does the company have a strategy that uses its strength in relation to competitive industry forces, thus improving the firm's relative industry position?

On analysing companies' relative valuations using comparable company analysis, intrinsic value compared with price using DDM and DCF, as well as 'softer' analysis, you can select which stocks best fit your portfolio's investment objectives and philosophies.

ASSET WEIGHTINGS

Once you define the asset allocation for your portfolio and select individual assets, you must decide on the weightings of the assets within your portfolio.

There are many different approaches for your investment weightings. There are simple theories, benchmark-based theories and advanced mathematical theories.

As with almost all aspects of investing, the weightings should be driven by your investment objectives and philosophies. The simple rule of thumb is to invest a higher percentage of your portfolio in assets you expect to outperform your benchmark.

One goal is that your basket of investments will outperform the overall basket of the assets. For example, your fund's investments in stocks would ideally outperform the overall stock market.

It is important to note that your analysis and valuations may be absolutely perfect, but if the market is valuing different characteristics, anticipating different events, or has different objectives and philosophies, the performance of your fund will not reflect your insight. As the charts in 'VALUE INVESTING' on page 71 and 'GROWTH INVESTING' on page 73 highlight, the market generally follows certain strategies, but it isn't always consistent.

Importance: There is a strong relationship between the economy and the stock market. Typically, the stock market acts as a leading economic indicator of the business cycle in an economy. Stock prices reflect expectations of company earnings, dividends and interest rates in the economy, and the stock market reacts to various leading indicator series.

Example: The following is a summary top-down analysis that will provide an overview of how the analysis can assist you with selecting equities that fit your desired asset weightings.

EXAMPLE: EQUITY SELECTION FOR ASSET WEIGHTINGS BY TOP-DOWN ANALYSIS

Let's say we set up Fund Example, a conservative growth fund, and we are going to select a portfolio of indices and stocks with the asset allocation of 30% indices and 10% stocks. This assumes Fund Example has already completed its asset allocation prior to asking us to select its equity investments.

As this is a conservative fund, we decide to focus on a few countries in the G7. We are looking for some diversity, so we select the USA, Germany, the UK and Japan. To analyse these countries, we identify a few economic indicators and financial metrics to get an idea of where we want to invest.

	USA	GERMANY	UK	JAPAN
GDP Growth	1.7%	0.1%	0.2%	0.5%
Div Yield	2.8%	3.9%	4.2%	2.2%
P/E	13.0×	10.5×	10.6×	14.5×

The aim is to select a few simple numbers which might tell us whether a market is cheap or expensive at any particular time. Two basic measures used are the P/E ratio and the dividend yield (DY).

GDP growth. The USA has experienced the greatest amount of GDP growth, over three times that of Japan, the next highest.

Dividend yield. The UK has the highest dividend yield, with Germany close behind.

P/E ratios. Germany and the UK have relatively low P/E ratios. The UK looks attractive with a high DY and low P/E.

The USA looks attractive with a high GDP growth rate and respectable DY and P/E.

Germany and Japan look attractive and very similar across all three metrics.

From this analysis, we decide to allocate the following across the countries:

	USA	GERMANY	UK	JAPAN
Invest %	40%	10%	40%	10%

Note: You can build a model to calculate these decisions on the basis of how important you feel the various economic and financial metrics are to the distribution of your investments.

As we are selecting for a conservative fund, we target a diverse set of industries that provide conservative growth. With your personal investment objectives and philosophies, you may decide to select different metrics to evaluate the industries.

	AUTO	PHARMA	SEMI	FOOD & BEV
Div Yield (%)	2.0%	3.8%	3.7%	3.0%
P/E	18.9×	15.8×	24.2×	40.3×
P/Book	1.5×	79.9×	3.7×	29.9×

Source: Yahoo Finance

Dividend yield. Pharma and semi look the most attractive from a DY perspective.

P/E. Pharma has the lowest P/E with food & bev having the highest.

Price/book. Auto and semi look attractive from a P/B basis, with pharma's very high P/B raising some concerns.

Pharma's high DY and low P/E ratio make it attractive, but the P/B raises concerns.

Semi looks attractive from a DY perspective and is reasonable across the other metrics.

Auto looks like a conservative investment based on its low P/B.

Food & bev looks less attractive than the other three.

	AUTO	PHARMA	SEMI	FOOD & BEV
Invest %	20%	40%	30%	10%

COMPANY ANALYSIS

We are most bullish on the pharmaceuticals industry and are therefore focusing on which stocks to purchase only in that industry.

	JNJ	PFE	ABT	NOVN
Div Yield	3.0%	3.3%	1.5%	3.4%
P/E	21.24×	23.1×	9.7×	18.0×
ROE	17.8%	11.6%	23.3%	14.1%

Source: Thomson Reuters

Dividend yield. NOVN and PFE are most attractive.

P/E. ABT appears undervalued relative to its peers.

Return on equity (ROE). ABT also appears to be generating the greatest return on equity for its shareholders.

	JNJ	PFE	ABT	NOVN
Invest %	0%	20%	50%	30%

ASSET WEIGHTINGS

On the basis of the analysis, we decide to invest in both geopolitical and industry indices. We like each of the options equally and decide to weight our investments equally between the two index types. With 30% to invest in indices, we invest 15% in geopolitical indices and 15% in industry indices.

We are most bullish about the pharmaceuticals industry and decide to invest all of the 10% allocated for stocks in the two companies that best fit our investment objective and philosophy.

INDEX	% OF FUND	STOCK	% OF FUND
USA	40% × 15% = 6%	PFE	20% × 10% = 2%
Germany	10% × 15% = 1.5%	ABT	50% × 10% = 5%
UK	40% × 15% = 6%	NOVN	30% × 10% = 3%
Japan	10% × 15% =1.5%		
Auto	20% × 15% = 3%		
Pharma	40% × 15% = 6%		
Semi	30% × 15% = 4.5%		
Food & Bev	10% × 15% = 1.5%		
Total	30%	Total	10%

COMPARABLE COMPANY ANALYSIS

Definition: Comparable company analysis is an extremely popular way to determine a company's relative value. The theory behind it is simple: if two companies are almost identical, their values should be almost identical. If they aren't, one company is likely overvalued or the other undervalued, or both.

Peers are carefully selected to ensure there is enough commonality to make the analysis relevant. The companies are all in the same industry, are roughly the same size, have experienced similar historical growth, and have roughly similar operating margins.

In practice, no two companies are identical, so comparable company analysis is an overview of several companies in the same industry presented in a way where it is easy to evaluate how the companies are performing and how they are valued relative to their peers.

When comparing companies, you will use the same valuation multiples mentioned earlier. These multiples compare the way the industry is valued relative to its financial performance. The most common multiples are P/E, dividend yield, market capitalisation/revenue, enterprise value/operating income (EBIT or EBITDA), and enterprise value/revenue.

You will also want to use the ratios that are more specific to your investment philosophies. For example, if you focus on growth, a common ratio used is the price of the company's stock compared to its earnings per share, which is then compared to its growth rate. The ratio is called the PEG ratio and is calculated by taking the P/E ratio and dividing it by the growth rate. There is a theory that the PEG ratio should equal one, and if it is greater than one, then it may be overvalued – and if it is less than zero then it may be undervalued.

Importance: What makes this analysis important is that it identifies investment opportunities and doesn't attempt to calculate the intrinsic value of a company or determine what the price of the stock should be. This is also the weakness of the analysis as it doesn't identify what the value of a company is; it just determines whether or not the value is in line with its comparable companies. If the industry is overvalued, it will misrepresent investment opportunities.

The optimal use for comparable company analysis is for investors who can adopt a hedging strategy, where you are able to go long on the stocks trading below the industry average and go short on those trading above the industry average. This way, even if the industry is overvalued and all stocks drop, you can expect that the stocks you have shorted will drop more than the stocks you have purchased, giving you a profitable outcome.

Example: The next table shows a comparable company analysis from 2010 that analyses companies in the internet information provider industry. For each company you can see the following information:

- Market cap (abbreviation for market capitalisation), which is the price per share multiplied by the company's shares outstanding. This gives you an indication for the size of the company.

- EV (abbreviation for enterprise value), which is the market cap of the company plus all of the debt the company has outstanding minus any cash it has in its accounts. This is the value of the market value of the company's equity and the value of all of the debt it has outstanding. Cash is subtracted from this value because the company generally has the option to purchase back debt whenever it likes. The reason EV is used is that it shows the value of all of a company's investors (equity and debt).

- Revenue multiple. The revenue multiple is calculated using EV/revenue and shows how the market values the company relative to its revenue. The columns CY10 and CY11 are for calendar year (ending in December) 2010 and 2011. The reason the calendar year is used is that companies report based on their fiscal year ending, which for most companies is in December, but there are many companies that prefer to report with a different month end. This is often influenced by industry factors: for example, many retail companies report their fiscal year end in January as they are generally busy with Christmas sales in December. In this example, CY10 are historical numbers, meaning the company has already reported its numbers, and C11 are projected numbers, meaning an analyst has estimated how the company will perform in the next year.

- EBITDA multiple. The EBITDA multiple is calculated using EV/EBITDA. EBITDA stands for earnings before interest, taxes, depreciation and amortisation. EBITDA is often the same as operating income, but sometimes there are subtle differences. This multiple is commonly used as it shows the value of the company relative to its core operations and disregards factors such as how the company has financed its operations, which affect interest, taxes, depreciation and amortisation.

- P/E multiple. The P/E multiple is the price per share divided by the earnings per share (EPS). In this analysis, where C10 is historical and C11 is estimated, the current price is used for both columns, but the EPS will differ. For C10, the historical EPS is used and for C11 the EPS estimate is used. The EPS estimate can be from one analyst. More commonly an average EPS is used from all of the analysts that provide estimates.

Select public company comparables – valuation statistics

Sorted by CY2010 EBITDA multiples ($ millions)

COMPARABLE COMPANIES ANALYSIS			REVENUE MULTIPLE		EBITDA MULTIPLE		P/E MULTIPLE	
COMPANY	MARKET CAP	EV	CY10	CY11	CY10	CY11	CY10	CY11
Selected Internet Comparables								
The Knot, Inc.	$279.0	$154.6	1.4×	1.3×	15.8×	9.4×	68.2×	31.8×
Travelzoo Inc.	267.8	235.8	2.2×	2.0×	11.3×	11.5×	28.2×	25.0×
Google Inc.	165,938.3	135,879.3	6.5×	5.6×	10.8×	9.3×	18.8×	16.1×

Yahoo! Inc.	20,417.2	16,788.6	3.6×	3.5×	10.2×	7.9×	25.0×	22.4×
Tech Target, Inc.	257.8	180.0	1.9×	1.7×	9.0×	7.3×	22.1×	18.0×
Answer Corp.	66.6	42.3	2.1×	NA	8.0×	NA	20.0×	NA
QuinStreet, Inc.	458.8	386.2	1.1×	1.0×	10.2×	4.9×	12.9×	11.8×
AOL Inc.	2,488.6	2,166.0	0.9×	1.0×	2.8×	3.2×	5.2×	8.3×
75th Percentile			2.5×	2.7×	11.0×	9.4×	25.8×	23.7×
Median			2.0×	1.7×	10.2×	7.9×	21.0×	18.0×
25th Percentile			1.3×	1.2×	8.7×	6.1×	17.3×	13.9×
Isis	$518.4	$459.7	4.0×	3.4×	9.6×	8.0×	25.8×	19.4×

The comparable company analysis example is from Jefferies and was used for the acquisition of Isis.

DIVIDEND-DISCOUNT MODEL

Definition: The dividend-discount model (DDM) is a widely-used valuation technique. It calculates a stock's intrinsic value based on its projected dividends.

The model is very simple: the stock's value equals the discounted value of the future dividend payments. It is the same theory used for valuing bonds.

Importance: This model provides a very quick valuation and works very well for mature companies with a stable customer base, predictable earnings and a commitment to paying out a stable stream of dividends. In these cases, the calculation for the present value of dividends is relatively simple:

Value of stock (DDM) = dividend per share ÷ (discount rate - dividend growth rate)

- **Dividend per share** is the expected dividend payable in one year.
- **Discount rate** is the required rate of return, which is the risk-free rate plus a risk premium, depending on the risk of the company being able to pay the dividend.
- **Dividend growth rate** is the expected increase of the dividend payments over time.

This model is difficult to apply to stocks that don't pay dividends, but it is not impossible. Some analysts include assumptions on what a company would pay for dividends, if it did pay dividends, based on its net income and cash flow.

As such, some have modified the model to include a short-term high-growth phase followed by long-term slow growth.

REQUIRED RATE OF RETURN

Investors require compensation for risk, in the form of increased expected returns.

It is important to understand the risks associated with an investment and your potential exposure to loss to determine whether you are being fairly compensated.

The required rate of return on an asset is the rate of return that investors expect (or require) to be induced to hold the asset. The required real rate of return is the extra return over and above the return on Treasury bills that the asset is expected to yield:

Required rate of return = risk-free rate + risk premium

- **Risk-free rate.** The appropriate risk-free rate is related to the investor's holding period. This could range from the yield on a three-month Treasury bill to the yield on a long-term government bond. For the DDM, you should use the 30-year Treasury yield.

- **Risk premium.** The risk premium that investors require from an asset depends on the asset's riskiness, as well as the investor's level of risk aversion (extremely risk-averse investors require extremely high risk premiums, which translates into the need to be compensated for holding risky assets).

ESTIMATE DIVIDEND GROWTH RATE

Estimating the dividend growth rate for a company is difficult, but extremely important to this valuation. What makes the estimate difficult is that the model assumes the growth rate will continue into the foreseeable future and very few companies can sustain a consistent earnings growth that can support dividend payouts over decades. It is not uncommon to have a company grow its dividend payments at a higher rate as it is still growing and pay out at a flatter growth rate once it has matured.

The growth rate of dividends can be estimated based on historical trends as well as calculated based on a company's ROE and its retention rate.

Historical growth calculation. Extrapolate past dividend growth to determine a company's dividend policy. This will provide you with a good estimate of how the company grows their dividend. This historical growth should be compared with long-term historical growth rates to determine whether the company's dividend policy is sustainable.

If the company's historical growth rate is much larger than the historical growth rates of similar companies in its industry then you will want to consider whether it will be able to continue to grow the dividend at the same rate in future.

$$g \quad \sqrt[3]{\frac{28.5}{5}} - 1 = 0.058$$

Likewise if the company's historical growth rate is much larger than the 5.8% growth rate experienced by the S&P 500 during the past 31 years, then you may want to consider its sustainability.

Example: The following example is a DDM sensitivity analysis where the discount rate is estimated between 8% and 12% and the dividend growth rate is estimated between -0.3% and 7.7%. At the time of this analysis, the stock was trading at $40.24. This analysis is useful for investors that place a lot of value on dividend payments to determine if a stock is overvalued or undervalued based on the implied assumptions.

At the current price, if you invest based on dividends, you have to be comfortable that the dividend growth rate will remain at 5.7% and that the discount rate of 8% is acceptable. If these assumptions hold true, the stock's calculated value from DDM is $41.74. If you aren't comfortable that the 5.7% dividend growth is sustainable or you require a larger discount rate, then the stock is overvalued. If we look at the middle of the assumptions (3.7% dividend growth rate, 10% discount rate), the model values the company at $29.45 compared to the current price of $40.24.

ASSUMED DISCOUNT RATES OF 8–12%					
DIVIDEND GROWTH RATE	**DISCOUNT RATE**				
	8.00%	**9.00%**	**10.00%**	**11.00%**	**12.00%**
−0.30%	$32.61	$28.37	$25.18	$22.68	$20.67
1.70%	$35.43	$30.76	$27.24	$24.49	$22.28
3.70%	$38.47	$33.33	$29.45	$26.43	$24.00
5.70%	$41.74	$36.09	$31.83	$28.51	$25.84
7.70%	$45.25	$39.06	$34.39	$30.74	$27.82

Source: myfijourney.com

The analysis highlights that the appropriate discount rate needs to be at 8% and the dividend growth rate needs to be above 7.7% for this to be a good investment.

DISCOUNTED CASH FLOW

Definition: The DCF model is used across many assets and is the most common way to value an investment, since it matches the expected cash returns with the investment or price of the asset.

For a stock, the DCF valuation is the present value of operating free cash flows. This model is very similar to the DDM, but instead of calculating the present value of all of the expected future dividends, the DCF calculates the present value of all of the future cash flow that a company is expected to generate. The discounted value of all future cash flow is the value of the whole company. As the value of a company is split between those that own its equity and those that own its debt, the value of the debt needs to be subtracted from the discounted value of all of the future cash flow to calculate the value of the company that the equity holders own. The cash available in the bank for the company is added to the value as it could be used to either buy back the debt or be paid to the equity holders.

DCF value(equity) = discounted(future cash flows) - debt + cash

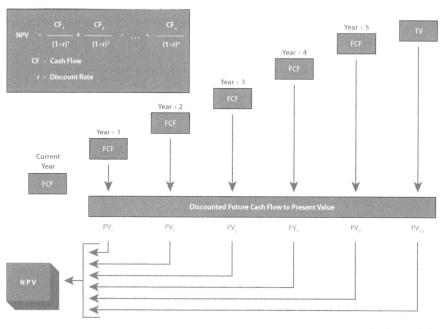

Source: valuationapp.info

To determine how a company's price compares with the value of the company determined by the DCF, you need to divide the DCF value(equity) by the company's current shares outstanding:

Compare stock price with [DCF value(equity) ÷ shares outstanding]

If the stock price is greater than the DCF value then it is overvalued. If the stock price is less than the DCF value, then it is undervalued. If the two are equal, then it is fairly priced.

Importance: DCF analysis is considered the most acceptable form of valuation, as it is based on the future performance of a company and the cash it will generate for investors.

Since the dotcom bubble burst in the early 2000s, equity research analysts have been required to include a DCF analysis in their reports to justify their valuations and recommendations. This change allows potential investors to evaluate the model and decide whether the analyst's assumptions are realistic.

Example: Below is the DCF for a publicly-traded company that Jeffries investment bank produced for a company that was deciding whether to make an acquisition. The analysis was filed with the Securities and Exchange Commission and is available to the public. To build this sort of analysis, investment bankers:

- **Project the future performance of the company.** The investment banker will build a projected model to estimate the future performance of the company. These models are generally available from research analysts if the company is publicly-traded. The purpose of this analysis is to estimate the free cash flow that will be generated by the company.

- **Calculate the weighted average cost of capital (WACC).** The investment banker will also calculate the interest rate that the company requires for investments. The purpose for deriving the WACC is to come up with the discount rate the banker will use to discount future cash flows.

- **Assume a terminal growth rate.** The terminal growth rate is used to estimate the free cash flow that will be provided beyond the projections available in the model. As the company will continue to exist, the banker will make an assumption on the appropriate terminal growth rate to calculate a terminal value. It is calculated by multiplying the final year's free cash flow by (1+growth rate) and dividing that value by (discount rate or WACC - terminal growth rate).

- **Calculate the enterprise value by discounting the cash flow.** Now that the banker has projected the free cash flow and calculated the terminal value for the company as well as the discount rate, the enterprise value can be calculated for the company. The enterprise value is calculated by discounting the free cash flow for each year, including the terminal value, back to today's date.

- **Adjust the enterprise value to derive a price per share.** After the enterprise value is calculated for the company, the banker will need to make adjustments to get to a price per share amount. The first step is to adjust from the enterprise value to the equity value. To do this, you need to add the cash and subtract the debt. In this example, the banker also added back the other benefits that the company will recognise in future, which include the present value of the net operating losses, which will reduce future payment of taxes (noted as PV of NOLs). Once the equity value is calculated, the banker divides by the diluted shares outstanding to calculate the price per share.

- **Build sensitivity analysis.** The DCF includes two major assumptions, which affects the price per share: the discount rate (or WACC), which affects the present value of the future cash flows, and the perpetuity growth rate, which affects the terminal value of the cash flows. Looking at the example, the sensitivity analysis looks at what the price per share would be if the WACC was between 11% and 15% and if the perpetuity growth rate was between 4.5% and 6.5%. In the extremes of the sensitivity table for the stock price, the price can vary from $7.56 to $14.24. This is designed to show you the best-case and worst-case scenarios and should raise questions about how comfortable you are with the assumptions.

ILLUSTRATIVE DCF VALUATION ($MILLIONS)	CY11E	CY12E	CY13E	CY14E	CY15E
Free Cash Flow					
EBITDA	$57.5	$66.6	$75.7	$84.3	$92.4
Less: Depreciation	(2.8)	(3.9)	(5.0)	(6.0)	(7.0)
EBITA	$54.7	$62.7	$70.8	$78.4	$85.5
Less: Taxes @ 35.0%	(19.2)	(21.9)	(24.8)	(27.4)	(29.9)
Add: Depreciation	2.8	3.9	5.0	6.0	7.0
Less: Capital Expenditures	(31.9)	(27.8)	(28.8)	(27.3)	(28.4)
Free Cash Flow	**$6.4**	**$16.9**	**$22.2**	**$29.6**	**$34.1**

PERPETUITY GROWTH RATE	
Weighted Average Cost of Capital	12.0%
Net Present Value of Free Cash Flow	$76.6
Terminal Growth Rate	**6.5%**
Terminal Value	**$661.1**
Present Value of the Terminal Value	397.0
Enterprise Value	**$473.6**
Add: Cash	58.7
Less: Debt	0.0
Prior Tax Benefits	41.6
Equity Value	**$573.9**
Divide By: Diluted Shares	47.8
Price Per Share	**$12.01**

PRICE SENSITIVITY ANALYSIS

		WACC				
		11.0%	12.0%	12.5%	14.0%	15.0%
PERPETUITY GROWTH RATE	4.5%	$10.90	$9.72	$9.26	$8.12	$7.56
	5.0%	$11.53	$10.17	$9.65	$8.38	$7.77
	5.5%	$12.27	$10.69	$10.10	$8.67	$7.99
	6.0%	$13.16	$11.30	$10.61	$9.00	$8.25
	6.5%	$14.24	$12.01	$11.21	$9.37	$8.53

EQUITY VALUE SENSITIVITY ANALYSIS

		WACC				
		11.0%	12.0%	12.5%	14.0%	15.0%
PERPETUITY GROWTH RATE	4.5%	$520.1	$462.6	$440.2	$385.1	$358.0
	5.0%	$550.5	$484.4	$459.2	$397.8	$368.0
	5.5%	$586.4	$509.7	$480.8	$411.9	$379.0
	6.0%	$629.4	$539.1	$505.8	$427.7	$391.3
	6.5%	$682.1	$573.9	$535.0	$445.7	$405.0

CHAPTER 11.
BOND SELECTION

OBJECTIVES

1. **Understand the principles behind debt valuation, specifically the time value of money and discounted cash flow.**

2. **Grasp the relationship between a bond's price and its yields.**

3. **Learn the core terms to describe bonds.**

BOND SELECTION PROCESS

Definition: The bond selection process varies by the type of bonds you include in your investible universe. In the case of corporate bonds, the process would be very similar to the equity selection process described in chapter 10.

In this chapter, bond analysis will be limited to risk-free bonds, specifically US Treasuries. This makes the analysis much easier, since there is much less concern about the US government defaulting on its loans than a corporation (the 2011 downgrade of the US government credit rating does raise some questions about whether the debt can still be considered risk-free, but for our purposes we will consider it to be as risk free as we will find).

The bond selection process focuses on bonds' absolute values using the discounted cash flow (DCF) model and the relative valuation of bonds using the yield curve.

Investment Selection - Valuation Analysis

BOND ATTRIBUTES

The bonds discussed here are US Treasury bonds.

The cash flows are coupon payments. Coupons are the payment amounts agreed by the bond issuer to be paid to the bondholder on set days over the life of the bond. Not all bonds have coupons; those that don't are called zero coupon bonds.

Face value payment is the amount that will be paid to the holder when a bond matures.

A bond's price and yield are determined by the market. There is an inverse relationship between the price and the yield. If the price increases, the yield falls, and if the yield rises, the price falls.

Price changes occur because of supply and demand for the bonds in the market. Yield changes are due to inflation, risk and any other factors that alter the interest rate required by the market to invest in a bond.

Importance: It is important to compare bonds' traits against your investment objectives and philosophies to determine which bond, or bonds, best fit your portfolio.

Example: The following is an example from the US government site about two different bonds. It shows the different pricing of the bonds based on the difference between the yield and coupon payment.

The simple rule is to compare the yield, which is the rate set by the market, and the coupon rate, which is set by the issuer. If the yield is greater than the coupon rate, then the price of the bond will be less than the face value of the bond. In the first bond, the yield is 4.35% and the coupon rate is 4.25%. This means the coupon will be less than what the interest payment would be for the bond. Therefore the purchaser of the bond will not pay full price for the bond, and will demand a price less than face value.

With the second bond, the yield is 3.99% and the coupon rate is 4.25%. This means the coupon will be worth more than what the interest payment would be for the bond. Therefore the purchaser of the bond will pay more for the bond than the face value.

HERE ARE SOME HYPOTHETICAL EXAMPLES OF THESE CONDITIONS:					
CONDITION	TYPE OF SECURITY	YIELD AT AUCTION	INTEREST COUPON RATE	PRICE	EXPLANATION
Discount (price below par)	10-year Note Issue Date: 8/15/2005	4.35%	4.25%	99.196069	Below par price required to equate to 4.35% yield
Premium (price above par)	10-year Note reopening* Issue Date: 9/15/2005	3.99%	4.25%	102.106357	Above par price required to equate to 3.99% yield

Source: www.treasurydirect.gov

DISCOUNTED CASH FLOW

Definition: One of the most straightforward assets to value is a government bond. A government bond promises to pay a series of coupon payments to the holder at annual (or semiannual) intervals, plus the repayment of the bond's face value at maturity. There is very little uncertainty in the promised income stream.

$$P_{0,n} = \frac{c}{1+r} + \frac{c}{(1+r)^2} + \dots \frac{F+c}{(1+r)^n}$$

Here $P_{0,n}$ is the price today of an n-period bond, c is the promised annual coupon payment, F is the face value that will be repaid to the holder of the bond at maturity, r is the investor's required rate of return, n is the number of periods the coupon is paid.

The investor's required rate of return will be the investor's opportunity cost of capital: it will be the rate of return that the investor could earn on a similar investment. Since a government bond is fairly secure, with little risk of default, the opportunity cost of capital will be the risk-free rate of interest. Although the eurozone crisis of 2010 saw some governments' ability to pay their debts called into question, their repayments were subsequently guaranteed by other European Union countries.

Further details on the required rate of return are discussed in chapter 10.

Example: The government issues an 8% five-year bond that pays its coupon annually. What is the price at which the government can sell the bond if the annual market rate of interest on safe assets is 9%?

Placing these numbers in the DCF formula looks like this:

$$P_{0,5} = \frac{8}{1.09} + \frac{8}{(1.09)^2} + \frac{8}{(1.09)^3} + \frac{8}{(1.09)^4} + \frac{8+100}{(1.09)^5} = 96.11$$

This price of $96.11 means that the coupon payments are less than what the market demands from a required rate of return. It is not willing to pay the face value of $100 for the bond.

YIELD CURVE

Definition: The yield curve is the common method of representing bonds graphically. The curve represents what the market's required rate of return is for bonds of different periods. In general, the longer the duration of a bond, the more an investor will demand for interest, but this isn't always the case. In the following chart, there are examples of the different scenarios of a yield curve.

A normal yield curve represents when investors expect higher interest rates for longer terms of investment. This occurs when money is theoretically tied up for a longer period and there is a greater risk in holding these longer-term assets since prices are more volatile.

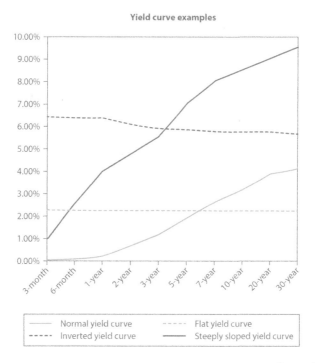

Yield curve examples

Source: bankrate.com

A flat yield curve represents when investors are indifferent between short-term and long-term investments. This occurs when there is less visibility into what will happen with the mid- to short-term rates as investors are just as fine locking into a long-term investment as a short- to mid-term investment.

The inverted yield curve represents when investors expect rates to be significantly lower in the mid- to long-term due to changes in monetary policy or changes in inflation and are willing to settle for lower rates for mid- to long-term investments.

The steeply sloped yield curve represents when investors expect rates to be significantly higher in the mid- to long-term due to changes in monetary policy or inflation and require a significantly greater rate of return for a long-term investment.

Importance: The yield curve is very helpful in selecting the investments that best fit your investment objectives and philosophies. Short-term bonds are safer than long-term bonds, since you can hold them to maturity without being affected by the price changes due to market conditions.

Long-term bonds guarantee coupon payments, but the price is more volatile due to the longer stream of coupon payments that are discounted back to determine its price. If there is a change in the yield due to market conditions, the short- and mid-term bonds will be less volatile than the long-term bonds.

If you expect the market to move from equities to fixed income, then the volatility will work in your favour when you hold long-term bonds. However, if the shift moves in the other direction, it will create a greater loss for your fund.

Example: The next figure is a chart from the US Treasury showing the comparison of two yield curves, one from the end of Q1 1999 and the other from the end of Q1 2013. Both curves are what is referred to as normal yield curves, meaning the short-term bond yields are less than the long-term bond yields. The difference between the curves is the slope of the curves. The yield curve from 1999 is much flatter than the curve from 2013. A flatter yield curve indicates that investors don't expect short-term rates to change much in the future; a steep yield curve indicates investors expect change or see greater risk in the bond market in future.

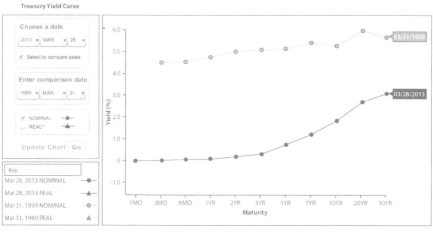

Note: X-axis (maturity) is not to scale

In 1999, the internet bubble was still growing and there was more demand for stocks than bonds – hence the yield curve in 1999 shows a much flatter curve.

SAMANTHA: ADVISING CLIENTS ON FIXED INCOME

Samantha is always trying to decide how much of a client's portfolio should be held in fixed income instruments such as bonds and money market instruments.

The major advantage of fixed income instruments is in its name: they provide a nice, predictable stream of fixed income for investors.

A disadvantage of fixed income instruments is that on average they offer lower rates of return than equity instruments. In recent times, the rates of return for bonds and money market instruments have been close to 0%.

There is also a significant relationship between the bond market and the equity market. As the demand for equities increases, investors move their money from bonds and money markets to equities, driving prices of equities up, prices of bonds down, and yields for bonds up. The reverse is also true.

Samantha is always thinking about how to optimise her clients' portfolios on the basis of the market trends between stocks and bonds.

CHAPTER 12.
BUYING AND SELLING

OBJECTIVES

1. Understand the benefits and limitations of a market order and limit order.

2. Gain a basic understanding of the market theories.

3. Learn when you would want to use each in managing your portfolio.

4. Learn about transparent markets and dark pools.

BUYING AND SELLING

Definition: After you decide on your asset allocation, select equities and bonds, and define your weights in each, you need to buy and sell assets to build your portfolio to the specifications you have defined.

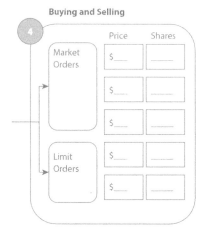

Buying and Selling

You will spend time creating a detailed plan to buy and sell your assets using different order methods, such as market orders or limit orders (explained later in this chapter). Each order type has unique benefits and limitations.

Importance: Buying and selling investments is an extremely important step, since all of your analysis to this point could go to waste if you don't properly execute your orders. You face the challenge of analysing in a static environment, then buying and selling in a dynamic environment. This means that the prices used in your analysis may not be the same as when you look to acquire your assets. Also, if you use limit orders, you may not end up with all or any of your orders executed.

Example: A fund manager wants to rebalance his portfolio by selling shares of an equity index and purchasing shares of stocks simultaneously. If a limit order is used on the sale of the index, the fund manager may not sell the shares of the index and end up with a portfolio that does not match what was designed to meet the investment objectives.

TRANSPARENT MARKETS

Definition: A market is transparent if all relevant information is fully and freely available to the participants of that market. Within financial markets, transparent markets are those where all information about the assets traded is available to investors, the details about the market participants are available, and the details about the transactions are available.

Asset information. Exchange commissions – for example, the Securities and Exchange Commission (SEC) in the USA – require all relevant information about an asset to be available for it to participate in the market. For the initial sale of an asset into the market, such as with an initial public offering or the sale of bonds, all relevant information is made available in a prospectus. The prospectus for an equity offering will have details about the company, its performance, the management team, ownership structure and risk factors, among many other things – all designed to enable people to asses the value of the company. The prospectus for a bond offering will have the terms and conditions of the bond – which includes the amount, when it will be repaid, the coupons it will pay out, the covenants the underlying entity must maintain, and many other details to assist with the valuation of the bond. After the initial sale of the assets, exchange commissions require the underlying entities to provide periodic details, such as annual reports, as well as event-driven reports, such as notices to the market of significant events that may affect the value of the assets.

Market participants. Exchange commissions require market participants to be licensed and meet various stringent requirements to be allowed to participate in the market. Transparency is vital: having a better understanding of a counterparty in a transaction is important for settlement reasons as well as to ensure false transactions aren't occurring just to manipulate the market. When looking at the equity market, almost anyone can purchase shares in a company, but those purchases will go through a firm that is licensed to purchase shares from the market. The unlicensed individual is not allowed to purchase directly from the market.

Market transactions. Exchanges also require the details of each transaction to be made available to market participants. These details include the buyer, seller, number of shares and price. In addition to completed transactions, market participants also make available the prices at which they are willing to pay for assets or sell assets into the market. Each market maker in a stock will post the number of shares he is willing to sell at a particular price – known as the 'ask' price. He will also list the number of shares he is willing to buy at a particular price – the 'bid' price. With each stock having multiple market makers, there are generally many bids and asks for a certain stock. The aggregation of these details is generally referred to as the 'order book' for an asset. These details won't allow the market to determine how many shares a market participant is ultimately planning to purchase, but it will indicate how much he or she is planning to purchase or sell next.

Importance: Transparent markets are at the foundation of a market-based economy. Transparency allows participants to accurately value assets, ensure transactions will be executed, and understand exactly how a transaction was executed. All of these measures are in place to build trust in the markets. Strong trust in the markets encourages active participation. With active participation, the markets will be more efficient and prices will better represent the value of the assets thanks to increased liquidity of the assets.

Example: NASDAQ's vision statement is "to be the best-performing, fairest, fastest, most transparent stock market in the world". The SEC's vision statement is "to promote a securities market that is worthy of the public's trust and characterised by: Transparent disclosure to investors of the risks of particular investments; Oversight of key market participants, including exchanges, brokers and dealers, municipal advisors, and others; Focus on strengthening market structure and systems; Promotion of disclosure of market-related information; Protection against fraud and abuse; and Evaluation, development and maintenance of appropriate rules and regulations."

At the very core of the two visions is transparency, in order to ensure US security markets are trustworthy.

DARK POOLS

Definition: Dark pools are exchanges that allow traders to buy or sell large orders without having to disclose the quantities they are interested in buying or selling. Not having to disclose the quantity of shares reduces the risk other traders will work out what they are doing and adjust prices to take advantage of the increased supply or demand of particular shares. Dark pools have been criticised for their lack of transparency and for being potentially less efficient than traditional transparent stock markets.

In dark pools, the amount of shares requested pre-trade, the type of order, and the prices set by limit orders are not visible to anyone, and the price at which shares change hands is only revealed after a trade is done.

Importance: The purpose of dark pools is to minimise the market impact of large buy and sell orders. The pools are available only to certain types of institutional investor in order to keep out undesirable participants.

Dark pools also potentially improve the price at which funds are able to buy and sell shares because transaction costs are reduced by transacting orders at the midpoint of quoted bid and offer prices. This is different from transparent exchanges, where purchases are made at the ask price and selling is done at the bid price. With dark pools, the buyers and sellers meet in the middle. This is another reason why dark pools have been popular for the execution of large orders.

Example: An example of a dark pool is SmartPool, the European dark liquidity pool created by NYSE Euronext in partnership with HSBC, J.P. Morgan and BNP Paribas.

LEO: BUYING AND SELLING

There is a trading floor within the investment firm that owns the fund that Leo manages. The trading floor helps Leo buy and sell securities for his fund, buying at the lowest possible price and selling at the highest.

Leo needs to make sure the traders know the highest price he is willing to pay for a stock. It would be a problem for Leo if he calculated the value of a stock at $10, all of his analysis was based on the prior closing price of $7, and the trader purchased the shares at an average price of $12.

One strategy the trader will use is to break up the purchase into smaller orders as large orders have the potential to significantly move a stock price. For example, placing a sell order for one million shares of a stock where there aren't a lot of buyers will be difficult to execute – the buyers will quickly start to drop the price they are willing to pay and some will not be comfortable buying when someone is selling such a large amount. There will be concerns that the seller knows something the buyers don't.

Leo will also speak to the traders to get an idea as to who is buying and selling within a particular stock, as traders generally have a good network and are a good source of rumours.

MARKET ORDER

Definition: A market order is an order to buy or sell a security at the price the market is willing to pay at the time the order is placed. This order type guarantees that the order will be executed, but it does not guarantee the execution price. The reason it can guarantee the execution of the order is that within the major exchanges there are market makers, which are banks that are required to state the price at which they are willing to purchase and sell shares within the market. The price they are willing to purchase shares for is known as the bid and the price they are willing to sell shares for is known as the ask.

The bid and ask prices are constantly changing and are influenced by the supply and demand of shares for a stock. For example, a market maker may be willing to buy 100 shares at $20/share, but if an order to sell 10,000 shares appears in the market, the market maker will only purchase the first 100 shares at $20 and will drop its price for the remaining 9,900 shares. This process guarantees there will always be a buyer and a seller in the market for an order, but the price will vary based on the supply and demand within the market.

Importance: Fund managers must remember that the last-traded price, which is the close price, is not necessarily the price at which a market order will be executed. If there is an excess demand in the market while the order is placed, the price will be greater than the last traded price. If there is an excess supply, the price will be lower.

Example: A fund manager wants to purchase shares of ABC Stock at the market rate and the prior close price was $10. If positive news comes out the night before the market opens, the fund manager may pay significantly greater than the $10 due to an excess demand for the stock.

LIMIT ORDER

Definition: A limit order is an order to buy or sell a security at a specific price or better. A buy limit order can only be executed at the limit price or lower (ceiling), and a sell limit order can only be executed at the limit price or higher (floor).

Importance: Fund managers must remember that they can set a limit on the price, but this does not ensure the order will be executed. The limit for selling may be too high and they may not find a buyer or only a buyer for a portion of their order. Likewise, the limit for buying may be lower than what the market is willing to sell at and the order may go unmet.

Example: A fund manager wants to purchase shares of ABC Stock for no more than $10. The fund manager could submit a limit order for this amount and this order will only execute if the price of the stock goes to $10 or lower.

Source: investor.gov/introduction-markets/how-markets-work/types-orders

CHAPTER 13.
MONITOR AND REBALANCE

OBJECTIVES

1. **Think about what you will monitor to ensure effective management of your portfolio.**

2. **Learn to monitor your portfolio and make adjustments to suit your management style.**

3. **Understand the needs of and methods for rebalancing your portfolio.**

MONITOR PORTFOLIO

Definition: Portfolio monitoring involves three major elements: market movements, new information and potential game changers. While there are other factors, we will only cover these fundamental ones here.

Importance: It is important to be aware of the various factors that can affect your portfolio's performance. Analysing changes to the performance of assets – as well as economic, regulatory and industry environments – is key to ensuring you are staying true to your original investment philosophy. It is very easy to spend time investing in the original analysis and not revisiting the analysis to ensure your existing portfolio is the portfolio you would have selected if you were to rerun the analysis today.

Example: Fund managers use various tools that assist them with their portfolio monitoring. Monitoring tools provide portfolio analysis, alerting, market data, aggregation of market-moving events and expert analysis. Some examples of companies that provide these services are Thomson Reuters, Bloomberg, FactSet, and S&P Capital IQ.

MARKET MOVEMENTS

Definition: The market movements you need to monitor are order executions, price movements and fund performance.

Order execution. You need to be aware of orders that execute, the price they execute at and how many shares are transacted, especially if you used limit orders. Getting the best price is an important part of maximising your returns.

Price movement. You need to be aware of price movements within your investible universe. It is important to analyse the biggest gainers and losers within this universe, identifying which ones moved the most and why.

Fund performance. You will continuously analyse how your fund performed on an absolute basis, relative to its benchmark, and relative to its peers.

Importance: Markets are dynamic and prices are always changing. The market may change based on perceived risks, overreaction to new information or favouritism for certain sectors. It is important to monitor these changes to ensure you are properly managing your portfolio and are comfortable with your decisions.

Example: When a stock price moves drastically up or down, it may provide an opportunity to analyse whether the market is overreacting to an event. If positive news drives a price significantly up and you own the stock, then you need to assess whether it is a selling opportunity based on the price being above your valuations. Likewise, if a stock drops significantly, it may be a good buying opportunity if the price is below your valuation.

NEW INFORMATION

Definition: Beyond price changes there is a constant flow of new information into the markets that drives these price changes. The main categories to monitor are relevant news, corporate performance, mergers and acquisitions, bankruptcies, stock splits, dividends, and country and industry changes.

Relevant news. News comes in many forms, whether it is a journalist breaking a story as it takes place and sending it though a real-time financial professional network, or a blogger spreading rumours about a potential acquisition. Portfolio managers need to try and monitor all of the relevant news available. As this is similar to trying to drink out of a firehose, the portfolio manager needs to develop ways to screen this information to break it down to the most relevant streams.

Corporate performance. In most countries, companies report their financial results either quarterly or semiannually. Companies also provide guidance throughout the year as well as announcements of significant developments. Additionally, equity research analysts are continuously updating their estimates for how they feel a company will perform in future. A portfolio manager needs to monitor these changes as they will affect valuation models and change perception on whether a stock should be within their portfolio.

Mergers and acquisitions. Companies acquire and divest other companies and divisions, respectively. When a public company announces it is being acquired or divesting a division, the announcement generally occurs while the market is closed as this gives investors time to calculate what the deal means to them. When publicly-traded companies are acquired it is generally at a significant premium to the trading price as the acquiring company usually has a strategic interest in the target companies. For example, the acquiring company can generally increase the revenue and/or decrease the expenses of the target company after it is integrated into the acquiring company. These increases in revenue and decreases in costs are the 'synergies' the acquiring company hopes to recognise as a part of the acquisition. It is important to note that, when a deal is announced, the acquiring company offers cash and/or stock to acquire the target company and once the market opens, the price of the target company will be at the offer price of the acquisition. Thus once the information is available in the market, the prior day's closing price is irrelevant to what the company is currently worth.

Bankruptcies. When a company is unable to pay the interest owed to its debtholders, it is generally forced into bankruptcy. Bankruptcy gives a company time to figure out how it will return to a state where it can meet its debt obligations. It may be that it needs to restructure its debt, bring in more equity investors (albeit at a significant discount for the investors), have the government bail it out, or sell off some of its assets. When a publicly traded company declares bankruptcy it is eventually removed from major exchanges, but this doesn't mean the stock stops trading. Once the company figures out how to satisfy its debtholders, it will exit bankruptcy and, if still public, will be eligible to be re-listed on the major stock exchanges.

Stock splits. Some companies decide to split their stock to keep its price within a certain range. For example, a company may prefer its stock to trade below $75/share and every time it trades to $100/share it will announce a stock split. This means that instead of owning one share at $100/share, you will own two shares at $50/share. The value of the shares is exactly the same, but because $50 is more affordable than $100, more individuals may purchase the stock, which will increase the price. This increase is generally due to investors feeling good about owning more shares or new investors being able to purchase more shares for a lower price

– but financially, it doesn't make a lot of sense. The value and ownership percentage will be exactly the same after the split as before the split.

Dividends. Companies that issue dividends generally have a dividend policy to provide clear visibility into future cash flows for investors. Companies try to increase dividends periodically to keep up with inflation and ideally represent the growth of the company's cash flow. Dividends are news when a company decides to start paying a dividend, a company decides to pay out a one-time extraordinary dividend, or a company announces it will no longer be able to pay its dividend. When these events occur, an investor will need to reassess his or her investment.

Country and industry changes. Changes to political and regulatory environments will have an affect on your portfolio and need to be monitored. The level of monitoring will vary according to the countries and industries where you are investing.

Importance: After designing your portfolio, you will need to monitor price movements and all new information to adjust your assumptions and valuation models to ensure your portfolio remains consistent with your investment objectives and philosophies.

What makes new information so important is that it provides insight into corporate performance and risk and can change outlook and projections for a company or country, which in turn will change your valuation models.

Example: When problems started to emerge in Greece back in 2009, some investors ignored the problem as they didn't own any assets in Greece. When the problem started to drag down the euro, creating concerns about Germany bailing the country out, and affecting trade between the USA and euro region, it began to change the assumptions of the markets and the way investors valued their assets. Those investors who were monitoring the situation and perceived the links between the crisis and their assets were more successful than those that didn't.

POTENTIAL GAME CHANGERS

Definition: There will be events that cause you to change the way you manage your portfolio. It is best to revisit your investment objectives, investment philosophies and investible universe periodically to ensure that what you originally set in place is still relevant.

Investment objectives. There are several reasons why an investment objective might change. A short-term milestone might be reached, the economy or a political event could change your perspective, or you could just be maturing as an investor.

These changes need to be recognised so that you can adjust your investment objective appropriately. This will change the fund's asset-allocation decisions.

Investment philosophies. Investment philosophies could change based on what is working within the market and what isn't. It is possible to imagine growth investors changing to value or speculative depending on whether their confidence in their abilities increases or decreases. However, it is usually advisable to stick with your philosophy; it is difficult to successfully chase market trends.

Investible universe. If a fund's investment objectives and philosophies change, it is conceivable that a fund will want to expand its investible universe.

Importance: You need to periodically confirm your objectives, philosophies and investible universe to ensure you are optimally managing your portfolio to achieve its goals. You should expect events to cause changes in the way a portfolio should be managed and it is important that you calibrate your fund as needed.

Example: After many years focused on aggressive growth, an investor may want to switch to a more conservative objective, focused on wealth retention. Instead of focusing on growth opportunities, the investor's philosophy could change to be more about value. The investible universe may also change as the focus will be less on individual stocks and more on indices and fixed income instruments.

LEO: BUILDING AND MAINTAINING HIS FUND

Leo manages an equity fund with a medium-sized investment management firm. He has a partner and the two of them focus on how to outperform their competition, which is generally noted as a 'benchmark', as well as how to attract more investors to their fund. Generally the two objectives work very well together because if they outperform their competition they will attract more investors – but that isn't always the case.

To outperform the benchmark, Leo and his partner rely on information from many sources, but it is ultimately up to them to decide where to invest. For example, Leo has a few research analysts who work for him researching ideas. Leo also has several friends that work for investment banks and are always promoting their clients' stocks, sending him research reports and detailed financial analyses. Many people refer to the information available to a portfolio manager as a 'mosaic' and they use their experience and knowledge of the market to interpret this information to make investment decisions.

To attract more investors, Leo and his partner pitch their performance and ideas for future investing to potential investors. As Leo wants to attract the

---

> most amount of money for every pitch, he will present to people who can direct the most amount of money to his fund. For example, Leo pitches his performance and ideas to Samantha as she has many wealthy clients that could be interested in his fund and she could persuade them to invest.

REBALANCE PORTFOLIO

Definition: Rebalancing a portfolio means buying and selling securities in a portfolio to reestablish original portfolio proportions for each asset class.

At the start of any investment programme, the fund manager sets an asset allocation by choosing to divide investment assets among a range of asset categories, usually including equities, fixed-income securities (bonds), cash and possibly some other assets. Ideally, he has analysed both his risk tolerance and risk capacity in order to set a sensible allocation (see 'ASSET ALLOCATION' on page 83 and 'INVESTMENT SELECTION' on page 83).

Through time, as asset prices change, the portfolio allocations will likely move away from the initial asset-allocation percentages chosen. As a consequence, the fund manager is now holding a portfolio with a different risk profile than initially decided upon. To correct this situation, the fund manager will want to rebalance the portfolio to bring it back to the original allocation structure. This process will involve selling assets in those categories that have increased in value and using the proceeds to purchase additional assets in those categories that have lost value. The goal is to return to the initial asset allocation percentages on a value-weighted basis.

Many fund managers tend not to be diligent in rebalancing. The reasons for not rebalancing are generally down to simple inertia, lack of time, intimidation by the process or any number of other excuses. Since the procedure requires taking money out of high-performing investments, which make up a larger percentage of the fund due to an increase in price, and reallocating the funds to weaker-performing assets, the process can seem counterintuitive to some. As such, the theory behind rebalancing the portfolio is sometimes delayed or ignored as the fund is performing well.

An opposite strategy of selling lower-performing assets to invest more heavily in top-performing assets, moving the allocation away from the original goal, is a high-risk strategy as the fund manager is effectively buying high-price securities in anticipation of prices going even higher, ignoring the original asset allocation defined by risk tolerance and investment goals.

A responsible fund manager will stick with the original asset-allocation decisions and rebalance on a scheduled basis or as the fund moves significantly away from the optimal allocation.

Importance: Rebalancing to your target asset allocation is necessary to keep your investments on course. This ensures that you are not overly exposed to a particular asset class if that asset class should suffer a bear market. It also forces you to adopt a strategy that is aligned to the classic 'buy low, sell high' method of investing.

Example: Target asset allocation: 60% stocks, 30% bonds, 10% cash.

Initial investment

	PERCENTAGE	VALUE
Stocks	60%	$60 mil
Bonds	30%	$30 mil
Cash	10%	$10 mil

Values one year later (before rebalancing)

	PERCENTAGE	VALUE
Stocks	63.7%	$65 mil
Bonds	26.5%	$27 mil
Cash	9.8%	$10 mil
Total	100%	$102 mil

Rebalancing required:

- sell: $3.8 million of stock
- buy: $3.6 million of bonds (the remaining goes to cash).

After rebalancing:

	PERCENTAGE	VALUE
Stocks	60%	$61.2 mil
Bonds	30%	$30.6 mil
Cash	10%	$10.2 mil
Total	100%	$102 mil

MARKET-CLASS

The expectations of life depend on diligence; the mechanic that would perfect his work must first sharpen his tools.

Confucius

CHAPTER 14.
MARKET-CLASS INTRODUCTION

OBJECTIVES

1. **Introduce the Market-Class simulation.**

2. **Explain the investible universe available to you.**

3. **Define your fund's objectives.**

OVERVIEW OF MARKET-CLASS

Market-Class is a portfolio-management simulation that immerses you in the experiences and challenges faced by portfolio managers. The simulation enables you to practise thinking and acting like a portfolio manager in an online, virtual, peer-to-peer environment.

You (or your team) will manage an active fund in a market and, alongside your peers, make regular investment decisions. All the data and news you need to make your decisions are within the simulator. Asset prices adjust based on the market participants' buy and sell decisions alone.

The following diagram explains the flow of the simulation.

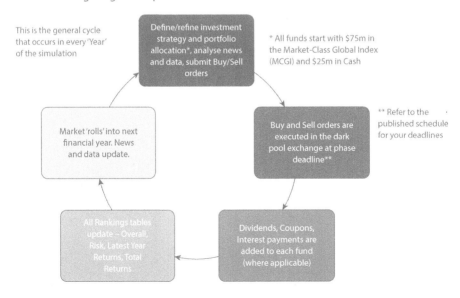

Use this book to help you structure your team, understand the traits of your investible universe, define your investment objectives, allocate your funds by asset type, select the individual assets, and buy and sell the assets.

MANAGEMENT OF AN ASSET PORTFOLIO

A major asset management firm has entrusted you to manage a $100m fund.

Your goal is to understand your investible universe, define your investment objectives, align your asset-allocation decision with the objectives, and select the individual assets that best meet your strategy.

The investible universe is made up of indices, stocks and treasury bonds. Although the funds are ranked based on a balance between the long-term capital appreciation, long-term volatility of the returns and short-term returns, the main purpose of the simulation is to ensure your fund's investment approach is consistent with your fund's investment objectives. Remember, not every investor wants the same return or risk from their investments.

As the manager of a fund you have the opportunity to make investment and rebalancing decisions periodically, such as every week. Every period within the simulation equals one year. At the end of every period, the prior period's closing prices will be posted, updated news events will be available, company financials will be updated, and fund performance details will be posted on the overview page as well as in the fund statement and fund report views.

STRUCTURING THE MANAGEMENT TEAM

You, the fund or management team, will focus on research and asset-allocation decisions. You and your team will decide who will take on key roles within the fund: portfolio manager, investment research analysts and dealing desk (traders).

Portfolio manager: The function of portfolio manager can be managed by a committee or an individual. The team should provide the manager input on key decisions, such as the fund's investment policy statement and asset-allocation decisions.

If a fund wants to have a single portfolio manager (either for the duration of the simulation, or on a rotational schedule), the team must define the responsibilities and basic framework for selecting which individual assets best fit the fund's asset-allocation model and investment style, based on recommendations by the investment research analysts.

Investment research analyst: A fund may want to assign different analyst positions, with each analyst focusing on a selected group of assets.

For example, one person could be assigned the auto industry and be responsible for identifying which companies are undervalued, which companies are experiencing the highest growth, how the industry's financials are changing and how they are affected by macro events. Ideally, the investment research analyst is able to rate each stock a 'buy', 'hold' or 'sell' for the portfolio manager.

The analyst will follow his or her industry over time, assessing valuations and altering recommendations as prices change and new financial information becomes available. This analysis will help the portfolio manager to decide which stocks in that industry, and what percentage, to hold.

The analyst may want to take on communications as well, advertising analysis and recommendations on the chat room and engaging in discussions on how the fund manager should be selecting stocks. The more the analyst is viewed as a thought leader within the market, the more likely the market will purchase shares the fund holds, which will help the fund outperform the market.

Dealing desk (traders). A fund may want to assign one person to be the expert on buying and selling assets, ensuring that orders are executed in a given period, are entered and match the parameters recommended by investment analysts – for example, whether to use market or limit orders and the quantities required.

FUND TYPE

The fund type you will manage as part of this simulation is a closed-ended fund (CEF), that is, you will not have to worry about investors in your fund. The $100 million assets under your management will not vary based on investors wanting to sell their investments in your fund, so you can better focus on a longer-term strategy without being concerned with having enough cash on hand in case investors sell up.

INVESTIBLE UNIVERSE

The investible universe for your fund includes one global index, four geopolitical indices, five industry indices, 25 equities, five Treasury bonds and cash.

The following is an overview of the majority of the assets held by the funds.

Geopolitical indices

Market-Class Global Index

Four regional indices:

Japan

UK

Europe

USA

All data in US dollars

Industry indices

Auto manufacturers

Food and beverages

Oil and gas

Semiconductors

Pharmaceuticals

All data in US dollars

Equities

Five companies per industry

Reference data

Balance sheet

Profit and loss

All data in US dollars

Bonds

Five Treasury bonds

1–30-year maturities

Fixed

Annual coupons

All US dollars denominated

MARKET-CLASS GLOBAL INDEX

The Market-Class Global Index (MCGI) is a market capitalisation (market cap) weighted index of the 25 equities within Market-Class. Purchasing a share of this index is equivalent to purchasing a fraction of a share of all 25 companies. The weighting of the shares you purchase is based on the size of the company, measured by its market cap. Index price changes are based on price changes of the 25 stocks.

All of the indices within Market-Class are calculated the same way the S&P 500 is calculated. The methodology employs divisor adjustments and is market-cap weighted. The detailed methodology is explained at: www.spindices.com/documents/index-policies/methodology-index-math.pdf

GEOPOLITICAL INDICES

There are four geopolitical indices: Japan, the UK, Europe and the USA.

These indices are market-cap-weighted indices made up of companies listed as doing business in the respective region. For example, the Japan Index (JPYI) is made up of all of the companies that are listed as Japanese companies.

INDUSTRY INDICES

There are five industry indices: auto manufacturers, food and beverages, oil and gas, semiconductors and pharmaceuticals. These indices are also market-cap-weighted, made up of the companies that are listed as doing business within the respective industries. For example, the Auto Manufacturers Index (AUTI) is made up of all companies that are listed as auto manufacturers.

EQUITIES

There are 25 equities and all are constituents (members) of an industry index, a geopolitical index and the global index.

Each company is included in the purchase of MCGI as well as the geopolitical and industry indices in which the company operates. For example, Nassan Cars (NSCJ) is a constituent of JPYI as it operates in Japan – as well as AUTI because it is an auto manufacturer, and MCGI because all companies are a constituent of MCGI. If a fund purchases 100 shares of JPYI, that purchase will translate into a purchase order for shares of Nassan Cars based on the weighting of Nassan's market cap as a percentage of the sum of all of the companies in JPYI.

BONDS

The bonds available are US Treasury bonds, which means they are as close to 'no risk' as possible – the likelihood of not getting paid back on the loan is close to zero.

At the beginning of the simulation, there are five bond options: bonds maturing in one year, two years, five years, ten years and 30 years. As the simulation progresses and these original bonds mature, more bonds are issued by the US government. For example, every year the one-year bond matures, paying the owner the coupon payment as well as the principal, and a new one-year bond is issued to the market.

CASH

There is the option to hold assets in your cash account. This account will yield the same rate of interest as the one-year Treasury yield and is as 'no risk' as the Treasury bonds.

CHAPTER 15.
OBJECTIVES AND RISKS

OBJECTIVES

1. **Define your fund's investment objectives.**

2. **Understand the risks you may encounter with your investments.**

3. **Set out your fund's investment philosophy.**

INVESTMENT OBJECTIVES

The investment objectives for your fund will be defined by your instructor, you or your team.

You or your team may want high performance, in which case the portfolio managers will want to focus on maximising total returns and reducing the volatility of the fund's performance year over year. You may decide that performance on the fund-ranking chart isn't a high priority and choose to measure the fund on the basis of different metrics, such as producing a consistent return every year, consistently outperforming the MCGI, the average fund's return or one-year Treasury bonds.

The important thing with setting investment objectives is that they are based on your investment policy statement and are the foundation for your investment-allocation decisions.

RISKS

Here is an overview of the risks and a summary on whether you need to be concerned about them within the Market-Class simulation.

Business risk: There is a business risk that needs to be considered when investing in companies as well as stock indices. A company may experience problems within its business. If this occurs it will be announced as a news item within Market-Class. Events that affect a company will be reflected in a change in its revenue and/or its profitability.

Market risk: There is a market risk that needs to be considered when investing in companies as well as stock indices. A market (geopolitical region or industry) can be adversely affected by macro events and these will be announced within Market-Class news. Events in a region or industry will affect every company within that region or industry and change its revenue and/or its profitability.

Financial risk: There is financial risk that needs to be considered when investing in companies as well as stock indices. Companies with significant fixed interest payments will have a more difficult time withstanding a turn in business performance or macro events than those with lower interest payments. This risk can be measured by analysing the income statements and balance sheets of the companies.

Liquidity risk: There is no issue with liquidity risk within the simulation as there is an active market for all investible assets.

Exchange-rate risk: There is no issue with exchange-rate risk within the simulation as all amounts are stated in US dollars and the financial and pricing values don't fluctuate with exchange rates.

Country risk: There is a country risk that needs to be considered when investing in companies as well as stock indices. A country (or geopolitical region) can be adversely affected by political events and these will be announced within the Market-Class news. Events that affect a geopolitical region will affect every company within that region and will be reflected in a change in their revenue and/or profitability.

INVESTMENT PHILOSOPHY

When selecting an investment philosophy for your fund you do not need to be restricted by only one. It is acceptable to base your decisions on one or two primary philosophies and keep some AUM set aside for more speculative or risky strategies.

CHAPTER 16.
MARKET-CLASS ALLOCATION

OBJECTIVES

1. Understand how to apply allocation and valuation theories to your Market-Class fund.

2. Select an asset-allocation model that works best for your fund based on its objectives and philosophies.

3. Understand how the Market-Class market works and how orders are processed.

4. Learn the difference between market order and limit order and how the orders are processed.

5. Learn how to place an order and capture the order rationale.

PORTFOLIO MANAGEMENT FRAMEWORK

The portfolio management framework will be the same for your fund as the one discussed in chapter 14. A larger view of the framework can be viewed in chapter 3.

MARKET-CLASS ASSET ALLOCATION

Your fund will start with an allocation of 75% in the Market-Class Global Index (MCGI) and 25% cash. Depending on how you want to manage your portfolio, you may want to select one of the following asset-allocation models or develop your own.

	CONSERVATIVE	MIDDLE	AGGRESSIVE
Stocks	5%	30%	80%
Indices	10%	20%	10%
Global Index	25%	10%	5%
Bonds	50%	30%	5%
Cash	10%	10%	0%

It is impossible to achieve the exact percentages you are targeting, as prices change between when orders are placed and when they are executed. The goal is not to maintain an exact allocation percentage within your fund, but to use an allocation model as a guide.

CASH AND MARGIN

Each fund starts with 25% of its fund in cash. When a fund acquires assets, the simulation checks to ensure there is enough cash in the fund's account to cover the estimated purchase price or that there are already orders to sell assets in place where the estimated proceeds cover the estimated purchase price of the assets.

If the actual purchase price of the assets is greater than the cash in the fund's account and the actual sale price of the assets, a margin account is set up for the fund. A margin account is where the bank lends the fund money, using the assets in the fund as collateral. The fund will pay interest for this money at a rate of 1.5% over the short-term bond rate.

If there is a positive balance in the cash account, that amount will earn interest at the same rate as the one-year Treasury bond.

MARKET-CLASS EQUITY SELECTION

You may adopt any equity-selection process you choose. The method recommended is the top-down analysis defined in chapter 15.

MARKET-CLASS BOND SELECTION

The method of bond selection recommended is to evaluate bonds based on yields, coupons and your fund's required rate of return.

MARKET-CLASS BUYING AND SELLING

Buying and selling assets within Market-Class starts with the order form and finishes with the execution of the orders via the market-making algorithm.

MARKET-CLASS MARKET PARAMETERS

Market-Class orders are executed within a dark pool that allows portfolio managers to place both limit and market orders. Combined with its proprietary market-making algorithm, all orders are filled at realistic prices and market behaviour mimics the real world as closely as possible. The Market-Class exchange is based on two principles.

1. Portfolio managers' orders 'make the market'. Execution prices are set based on the limit prices of orders placed by buyers and sellers. Shares will be sold based on the supply and demand of the market.

2. In the absence of portfolio managers' orders making the market, the Market-Class algorithm will 'make the market'. This occurs when there is no fund buying shares when another fund wants to sell, or vice versa. The Market-Class algorithm will therefore buy and sell shares at a reasonable price based on the quantity demanded or sold. The change in the price from the prior close price is based on a few different variables depending on the asset type.

For stocks, the execution price is based on the excess supply or demand of the company's stock.

For indices, the execution price is based on the excess supply or demand of the indices as well as each constituent's stock.

For Treasury bonds, the execution price for an individual bond is based on the excess supply and demand for the individual bond as well as the excess supply and demand for all bonds.

News events related to a company, industry or geopolitical region only have an effect on the company's revenue growth and/or operating margin. The news itself does not have an impact on the stock price. The interpretation of the news by portfolio managers and their subsequent buy and sell orders affect the price. For example, if a company announces that it will grow net income at a far greater rate than expected, if the portfolio managers don't see this as a reason to purchase the stock, the price will not increase. Likewise, if all portfolio managers see this as a reason to purchase substantial shares, the price will increase substantially, beyond what you may see as a fair value.

Net demand or net selling of a bond affects the price of all bonds as well as the bond being traded. This is because bonds are linked and only vary based on when the instrument matures, which is when the face value of the bond is paid to the investor. If portfolio managers choose to shift their investments from stocks to bonds and most portfolio managers prefer three- and five-year bonds, the demand of bonds will drive all bond prices up and will drive the price of the three- and five-year bonds up a little more.

Orders are executed once per phase, that is, order execution is not real-time. It makes no difference when you submit your orders within a phase.

Here is an overview of a phase cycle in Market-Class:

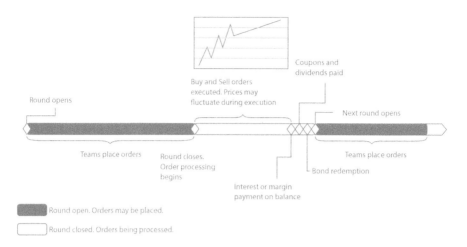

To explain what happens in the simulation, it makes sense to note that we are essentially combining two stages of the price change: (1) the change in price due to the purchase of the shares, and (2) the change in price over the remainder of the year due to the events and performance of the company – best accounted for by supply of and demand for the shares.

Since the simulation combines both stages into one (to simulate a year within a phase), it is not exactly what you would deal with during a year of trading in the real world. This is the best way we have found to represent the price change owing to market demand; it is the same scenario for all funds in the simulation.

To better manage the price and quantity of shares your fund acquires, Market-Class allows you to place market orders and limit orders.

MARKET ORDERS

A market order is always executed at the execution price, that is, at whatever price is determined by the market. A market order is always completely filled.

The following is an example of how the market order process works within Market-Class. The example shown is where one fund is selling 1,000 shares of a company at the market price and four funds are seeking to purchase the same stock at the market price. The buying and selling between the seller and buyers occurs at the prior closing price of $10. As there is greater demand from the buyers than there are shares being sold, the buyers will need to purchase additional shares from a market maker in order to fill their orders. Because of this excess demand, the market-making process results in prices rising based on the (excess) quantity of shares demanded from the market.

Note: The prices in the example are indicative of how the prices will increase and aren't actual outputs from the simulation.

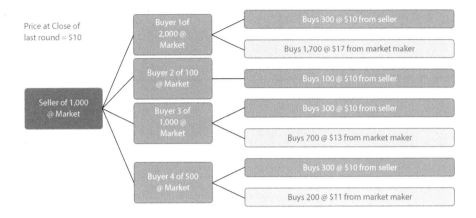

Key points:

- Fair distribution of the seller's shares.

- Excess demand and supply is met by market-making algorithm.

- The more shares ordered, the higher the volume-weighted average price (VWAP).

The following figures give an overview of how the orders are met for each fund purchasing shares. Both examples highlight that if your fund is buying and there aren't as many funds selling, the purchase price will differ based on the quantity of shares. If your fund is purchasing more shares than another fund, your average purchase price will be greater than the other fund.

Three portfolios place orders to purchase Company A.
Portfolio 1 buys 1,000 shares; Portfolio 2 buys 2,000 shares; Portfolio 3 buys 3,000 shares

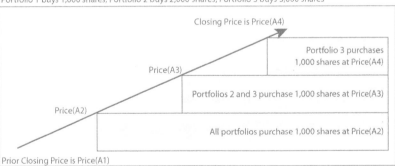

Portfolio 1 buys 1,000 shares at A2
Portfolio 2 buys 2,000 shares at a weighted average of (A2 + A3)/2
Portfolio 3 buys 3,000 shares at a weighted average of (A2 + A3 + A4)/3

The next example demonstrates what happens with excess selling.

Three portfolios place orders to sell Company B.
Portfolio 1 sells 1,000 shares; Portfolio 2 sells 2,000 shares; Portfolio 3 sells 3,000 shares

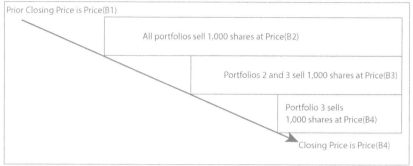

Portfolio 1 sells 1,000 shares at B2
Portfolio 2 sells 2,000 shares at a weighted average of (B2 + B3)/2
Portfolio 3 sells 3,000 shares at a weighted average of (B2 + B3 + B4)/3

LIMIT ORDERS

A limit order is an order with a price floor or ceiling. For example, if the close price of Stock A is $100 and you wish to buy that stock but not pay more than $125, then you would place a buy limit order at $125 for the quantity you wish.

Note that your order quantity may not get completely filled should the price exceed your limit in the execution process. Your statement page will show you how much you got filled and at what price.

The next figure is an example of how the limit order process works within Market-Class. A fund is selling 1,000 shares of a company with a limit price of $12.00, meaning the fund won't sell shares below that price. There are four funds seeking to purchase the same stock with varying limits. The buying and selling between the seller and buyers will occur based on whether the buyer is willing to purchase shares at the seller's limit price.

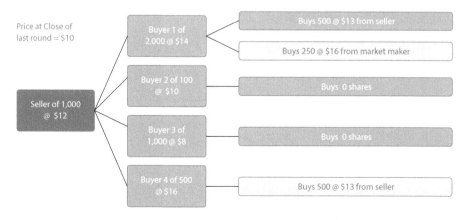

Buyer 1 has a limit order with a maximum price of $14.00, which means the buyer will purchase shares from the seller as the fund is willing to pay $14.00 and the seller is willing to accept $12.00. The two funds will settle the transaction at the price in the middle, which is $13.00. As Buyer 4 is also buying shares with a limit price greater than the selling price, the shares being sold by the seller will be split between Buyer 1 and Buyer 4 (500 shares each). As Buyer 1 has placed an order for 2,000 shares and has only purchased 500 from the seller, Buyer 1 will purchase more shares from the market maker until a weighted average cost of the shares is equal to the fund's limit of $14.00.

In this example, the fund was able to purchase 250 additional shares at $16.00, which is greater than the limit, but since 500 shares were purchased below the limit, the weighted average cost of all of the shares is equal to $14.00.

$$[(500 \text{ shares} \times \$13.00 + 250 \text{ shares} \times \$16.00) \div 750 \text{ shares}] = \$14.00$$

Buyer 2 and Buyer 3 have a limit order with a maximum price of $10 and $8.00, respectively. As these are both below the seller's minimum price of $12, Buyer 2 and Buyer 3 will not purchase any shares from the seller. In this example, there is excess demand for the stock, so the price will increase from the close price of the last period, so Buyer 2 will not end up purchasing any stock.

Buyer 4 has a limit order with a maximum price of $16.00. As Buyer 1 and Buyer 4 are the only two funds with a limit price greater than the seller's price, and their demand is greater than what the seller is willing to sell, the shares will be split between the funds at the $13.00 price set between Buyer 1 and the Seller. Buyer 4 ends up purchasing all of the shares demanded at $13.00.

Key points:

- The limit order defines the maximum or minimum VWAP a fund is willing to pay for or sell a stock.

- Not all orders are met and some are only partially met.

- Excess demand and supply is met by the market-making algorithm.

There is no prioritisation when it comes to a limit order as all orders are treated the same, but as prices rise above limits or below limits, the supply and demand changes. When prices rise above or below limit orders, there is less supply and demand in the market and what is generally left are the market orders as they will be executed at any price. So the limit orders are generally executed before the final market orders.

PLACING ORDERS

The order form page is where you submit your buy and sell orders. Go to the buy/sell column and click on the link for the asset you wish to buy or sell. The following order box will pop up:

The order form pop-up includes the following fields and options:

- close price of the asset (to provide an estimated transaction cost)
- your current holding of that asset
- order options
- market order
- limit order, which requires you to enter a dollar value
- buy or sell option
- quantity that you wish to buy or sell
- the estimated cost of your transaction, calculated based on the close price from the last year; this is estimated because the actual cost will only be determined as all orders are executed
- a warning message if your transaction exceeds the percentage holding rule or your fund does not have available cash to purchase the assets
- order rationale and the free text box (optional), which are discussed below.

ORDER RATIONALE

The order rationale is a way for a fund to track its asset-selection and rebalancing decisions. The rationale list is based on value investing, growth investing, event-driven investing and speculative investing. The 'other' option is provided as this list isn't designed to be comprehensive.

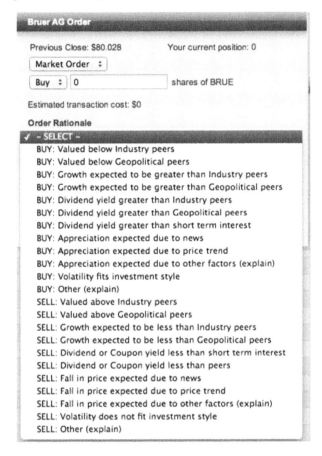

Select your order rationale and add notes to the free text field that accompanies the order form. The rationale and notes will allow you to easily analyse your investment decisions and determine whether the market agrees with your perceptions. If your fund purchases shares based on your analysis indicating that the stock is 'valued below industry peers' and the stock price increases at a rate greater than the market increase, you will know there is a good chance the other funds are valuing companies similarly to you. If you make the investment and the price underperforms the market, then there is a good chance the other funds are looking at other factors or have different asset-allocation preferences.

This knowledge may or may not influence your investment decisions or your postings in the chatroom. It is not uncommon for investors to promote their own analysis or insight to persuade others to invest in assets they hold so as to increase stock price performance.

BUYING AND SELLING INDICES

Here are details on how the transactions for indices (Market-Class Global Index, industry indices and geopolitical indices) work.

Buy and sell orders in the geopolitical indices and industry indices flow through as buy and sell orders in the constituents of the index, weighted by their free-float market capitalisation. The volume of shares traded in an individual stock will reflect the transactions within the indices in which the stock is included. For example, a stock that is a US auto manufacturer will have additional buy and sell orders if funds are buying and selling the US index as well as the auto index.

Industry index prices are determined by demand in underlying constituents. This eliminates arbitrage opportunities between indices and underlying stocks.

TRANSACTION FEES

There are no transaction fees within the simulation.

STATEMENT

Since the order-execution process is dynamic within the dark pool environment, actual obtained prices are likely to be different to previous and current close prices. Fund managers should carefully analyse their statement to understand what transaction prices are achieved and what quantities are filled (if a limit order).

MARKET-CLASS FUND PERFORMANCE

Your fund's annual performance will be based on (1) the change in price of the assets owned, (2) the price you receive for the assets you sell compared to the price of the assets at the end of the prior year, and (3) the price you acquire new assets for compared with the price of the assets' close at this year.

When there is excess demand for a stock your portfolio owns and you are acquiring more shares, the following process takes place.

Value of Company A Stock held in Portfolio Shares*Price(A1)	Purchase Shares	Price increase Price(A1) > Price(A2)	Dividends Paid	Cash	Value of Company A Stock held in Portfolio Shares*Price(A2)
	Order placed to purchase more shares of Company A. Increased demand for Company A drives the stock price up. The purchase price is greater than Price(A1).	The price increase to price(A2) The shares previously held will increase by the full price increase. The shares just purchased will increase by a reduced amount as the shares were	The dividends are paid for all shares held. The amount will appear as Cash within the portfolio.		

When an asset is being sold in the market there is pressure on the price.

Value of Company B Stock held in Portfolio Shares*Price(B1)	Sell All Shares Price(B1) > Price(B2)	Cash	
	Order placed to sell all shares of Company B. Increased supply for Company B drives the stock price down. The sell price is less than Price(B1).		The shares will be exchanged for cash may be used for purchases at the same time of the sell. Due to the sell order being executed below the prior opening price, the portfolio will experience a loss on the transaction.

MARKET-CLASS MONITOR AND REBALANCE

The rebalancing process starts with the decision on how the fund manager wants to allocate his or her assets for this year. It may help to think through the following tables.

A simple asset allocation within Market-Class can be used to guide the portfolio manager to rebalance the portfolio. For example, if the decision was made to stick to a 60/30/10 portfolio between stocks/bonds/cash and the performance of the stocks is far better than the performance of the bonds, then the portfolio manager will need to sell some of the stocks or indices and purchase more bonds.

	PERCENT	VALUE
Stocks	60%	$60 mil
Bonds	30%	$30 mil
Cash	10%	$10 mil
Total	100%	$100 mil

This may seem counterintuitive as the rebalancing process involves selling some of the higher-performing assets to purchase some of the lower-performing assets. The portfolio manager needs to decide if it is best to stick with the fund's strategy or deviate based on new information in the market. It takes a lot of discipline to stick with a philosophy and not be tempted based on what others in the market are doing.

There is likely a need to rebalance your portfolio after every period. Refer to the section 'REBALANCE PORTFOLIO' on page 126 to better understand how to rebalance your portfolio.

MARKET-CLASS FUND RANKINGS

The details required for analysing fund rankings are available in the individual asset 'tear sheets' under research as well as the 'fund performance' page, which is available within the simulator for each fund. Fund managers are able to view their performance details within the 'total returns and risk' section and the benchmark details in the 'market attributes' section. The benchmark can either be MCGI, which is the total return for the equity market, or the fund manager can use the all funds average total return, which is an average of the other funds within the market.

Performance is ranked on the basis of the performance of the other fund managers – your peers in the market.

Success is measured across three weighted dimensions:

1. latest-year return (25%)

2. risk (25%)

3. total return (50%).

Latest-year return is the percentage change in the value of your portfolio from the previous year. A ranking value is assigned to your fund based on the percentage return you achieved relative to your peers.

Fund volatility is the measure of risk of your fund relative to its peers, using a standard deviation calculation of the series of total returns you have achieved.

Total return is defined as the current value of your portfolio, ranked relative to your peers based on the US dollar value of your fund.

GLOSSARY

401(k) A 401(k) plan is a defined-contribution plan where an employee can make contributions from his or her pay either before or after tax, depending on the options offered in the plan. The contributions go into a 401(k) account, with the employee often choosing the investments based on options provided under the plan. In some plans, the employer also makes contributions, such as matching the employee's contributions up to a certain percentage. Some plans have mandatory employer-contribution requirements. Source: IRS (2014), www. irs.gov

Anticipated return The amount of cash flow one would receive from an investment.

Arbitrage The practice of taking advantage of price differences between financial instruments or markets to generate a guaranteed profit.

Asset allocation The process of apportioning a pool of money into different asset classes. The specific allocations applied will depend upon various factors – for example, an investor's preferences with regard to risk and reward.

Asset portfolio A group of assets – for example, cash, real estate, equities, bonds or commodities – that are owned by an individual or organisation.

Assets under management (AUM) The total market value of assets managed by an investment firm or portfolio manager.

Back office The name given to the part of an organisation – e.g. an investment bank – that deals with the administrative aspects of financial transactions such as settlements, valuation and compliance.

Benchmark The standard by which the performance of an asset, portfolio or fund manager is measured to determine its relative performance.

Benchmark portfolio A comparison standard of risk and assets included in the policy statement that are similar to the investor's risk preference and investment requirements, which can then be used to evaluate the investment performance of the portfolio manager.

Beta A standardised measure of systematic risk based upon an asset's covariance with the market portfolio.

Bonds   A debt investment in which investors loan money to the bond issuer who borrows the monies for a defined period of time and pays the investors a predetermined interest rate (known as a coupon).

Book value   The net asset value of a company, calculated by total assets minus intangible assets (patents, goodwill) and liabilities.

Buy side The aspect of the financial services industry that comprises the firms e.g. investment funds, private equity funds, hedge funds, pension funds, life insurance firms etc, that buy securities and assets for their own or their clients' accounts.

Capital asset pricing model (CAPM)   A finance theory concerned with deriving the expected or required rates of return on risky assets based on the assets' systematic risk levels.

Capital market line (CML)   The line from the intercept point that represents the risk-free rate tangent to the original efficient frontier; it becomes the new efficient frontier since investments in this line dominate all the portfolios on the original Markowitz efficient frontier.

Compliance officer   Manages the regulatory aspects of a firm or fund, and is responsible for general compliance – ensuring that all investment decisions and activities comply with client and legal mandates.

Dark pool   An off-exchange venue where trades are executed 'in the dark'. What this means is that the price, size of trade and seller are not advertised as they are in 'lit' venues such as an open exchange.

Discounted cash flow (DCF)   A technique, of which there are various versions, to value a stock based upon the present value of some measure of cash flow, including dividends, operating cash flow and free cash flow.

Diversification   Where an investor's pool of assets or investments is spread across a range of assets, asset classes or other asset characteristics in order to spread the risk and performance attributes.

Dividend discount model (DDM)   A technique for estimating the value of a stock issue as the present value of all future dividends.

Dividend yield (DY)   The ratio of how much a company pays out in dividends relative to its share price. The dividend yield is calculated as annual dividends per share divided by price per share.

Duration   A composite measure of the timing of a bond's cash flow characteristics, taking into consideration its coupon and term to maturity.

Earnings per share (EPS)   The value of earnings per each outstanding share of a company's common stock. It is generally calculated by dividing net income by the number of shares outstanding.

Earnings yield   The earnings per share divided by the share price, presented as a percentage.

EBIT   Earnings before interest and tax – an indicator of a company's profitability, calculated as revenue minus expenses, excluding tax and expenses.

EBITDA   Earnings before interest and tax, depreciation and amortisation – the same as EBIT but also removes the two non-cash items of depreciation and amortisation from the equation.

Enterprise value   Calculated as the market capitalisation of a company's stock plus its total debt outstanding, minus total cash and cash equivalents.

Expected risk   The risk of the anticipated returns from an investment not being realised.

Free float   Represents shares outstanding available for public investors, i.e. the number of shares not including restricted or privately-held shares.

Front office   The name given to the part of a business that is in direct contact with its customers and where revenues are generated, e.g. sales, marketing and corporate finance employees.

Fundamental analyst   An analyst who researches a company's operating performance and projects future performance based on industry, sector or company insight and expertise, with a view to recommending companies for portfolio managers' consideration.

GARP investing   Growth at a reasonable price – an investment strategy that is a hybrid of value investing and growth investing.

Gross domestic product (GDP)   A measure of aggregate economic output or activity.

Growth investing   An investment strategy that involves identifying and investing in companies or securities that consistently experience above-average increases in sales and earnings.

Growth stock   A security that generates a higher rate of return than other securities in the market with similar risk characteristics.

Hedge fund   A pooled investment vehicle administered by a professional management firm. Hedge funds are typically only available to accredited or sophisticated investors, not the general public, and therefore generally avoid direct regulatory oversight and licensing requirements – meaning that they can operate with greater flexibility than other investment funds.

Income statement   A financial statement that shows the flow of the firm's sales, expenses and earnings over a period of time.

Indices   A composite selection of securities that represents a particular market or portion of a market. Each index has its own composition and calculation methodology. In the Market-Class simulation, an index is a composition of the stocks from a particular region or sector, with each stock's weighting stated.

Inflation   A persistent increase in the general price level of goods and services in an economy over a period of time.

Initial public offering (IPO)   The first equity issuance to the public market by a company.

Investible universe   The entire range of assets or securities that are available, or are deemed suitable to be available, for an investor to invest in.

Investment horizon   The time period used for planning and forecasting purposes, based on the future point at which an investor requires invested funds.

Investment policy statement   A statement in which the investor specifies investment goals, constraints and risk preferences.

Investment trust   A form of collective investment and a closed-ended fund, established from the sale of a fixed number of shares launched from a pool of investors' money. Investment trust shares are traded on open stock exchanges like public companies.

Junk bonds   Also known as high-yield bonds – fixed-income instruments that pay a higher rate of interest because the risk of default is deemed higher than 'investment-grade' bonds.

Limit order   A buy or sell order that has a price limit set. For a limit buy order, the limit is the ceiling, or maximum price, meaning that the buyer is prepared to purchase the asset at a price up to the limit price. For a limit sell order, it is the floor, or minimum price, that the seller is prepared to sell an asset for. The purpose of a limit order is to protect the buyer or seller from executing at a price that they consider to be too high or low.

Liquidity   The term used to describe the ease with which assets can be bought or sold. A market with many active buyers and sellers would be deemed a liquid market. Equally, an asset that can be easily bought and sold may be termed a liquid asset.

Management fee   What a fund management company charges for the management of a portfolio or investments. The fees are usually either a fixed percentage, e.g. 0.5%, or are performance-related. A management fee is also usually levied for investments made on platforms that track established benchmarks or indices, e.g. the FTSE 100.

Margin   The percentage cost that a buyer has to pay in cash to buy an asset, where the amount they need to fully fund the transaction has been borrowed.

Market capitalistion   The value of a company's shares outstanding and tradable in the market. It is calculated by multiplying the number of shares outstanding by the current price of a share.

Market order   An order to buy or sell an asset at the price the market is willing to pay at the time the order is executed. This type of order is guaranteed to be executed but it does not guarantee the execution price.

Middle office   Describes the professionals who support the 'front office', i.e. portfolio managers, analysts and traders. The middle office typically comprises people dealing with the operations and technology of the business.

Modern portfolio theory   A finance theory that attempts to maximise the expected return of a portfolio given the amount of risk.

Mutual fund   An investment vehicle that comprises a pool of funds from many investors for the purpose of investing in securities. Mutual funds are managed by money managers, who invest the fund's capital with the goal of producing capital gains and income for the investors.

Net asset value (NAV)   The market value of an investment company's assets – e.g. securities, cash and any accrued earnings – after deducting liabilities, divided by the number of shares outstanding.

Net current assets   Calculated as current assets minus current liabilities. It indicates how much capital is being generated or used in the day-to-day workings of a business.

Over-the-counter (OTC)   A market involving the trading of securities which are not listed on an organised or formal exchange. In theory, any security can be traded on the OTC market as long as a registered dealer is prepared to make a market in the security.

Ponzi scheme   A Ponzi scheme is a fraudulent investment that promises high rates of return with little risk to investors. It produces returns for existing investors by acquiring new investors – the inflow of new money is paid out as returns to existing investors. When new investors fail to materialise, the scheme collapses.

Portfolio manager (or fund manager)   The person responsible for all aspects of the fund: its construction, investments, rebalancing – as well as the client relationship, i.e. the principle investors in the fund that they manage.

Price-to-earnings ratio (P/E)   The number by which expected earnings per share is multiplied to estimate a stock's value. Sometimes this is also referred to as the earnings multiplier.

Primary market   The market in which newly-issued securities are sold by their issuers who receive the proceeds.

Private equity   An equity stake in a company that is not traded on a stock exchange.

Quantitative analysts   Analysts who use computer-based and mathematical models to identify investment opportunities.

Required rate of return   The return that compensates investors for their time, the expected rate of inflation, and the uncertainty of the return.

Return on equity   Measures a firm's effectiveness at generating profit from every unit of shareholders' equity. It is calculated as net income divided by shareholders' equity.

Risk premium   The increase over the nominal risk-free rate that investors demand as compensation for an investment's uncertainty.

Risk-free assets   An asset with guaranteed returns, such as US Treasury bills.

Secondary market   The market in which outstanding securities are bought and sold by owners other than their issuers.

Sell side   The aspect of the financial services industry that is involved in the creation, promotion, marketing and selling of financial securities. Its goal is to sell its products and services to the buy side of the industry.

Sharpe ratio   A relative measure of a portfolio's benefit-to-risk ratio, calculated as its average return in excess of the risk-free rate divided by its standard deviation.

Sovereign wealth fund   A sovereign-owned investment vehicle that invests monies derived from its reserves to benefit the sovereign state or entity. They are typically created from a balance-of-payments surplus.

SWOT analysis   SWOT refers to analysing a company based on its strengths, weaknesses, opportunities and threats. It is generally represented on one page with each topic covered in a quarter of the page.

Top-down analysis   The process of starting with global or country analysis to identify how an investor might want to weight their portfolio. The process starts with the top level (region or country), then drills down into further levels (sectors), before selecting individual investments (stocks).

Tracker   Aims to mirror or 'track' the performance of an existing stock market index, e.g. FTSE 100, S&P 500.

Unit trust   Formed to manage a portfolio of securities in which investors can buy units.

Value investing   An investment strategy that involves identifying and investing in companies or securities that appear to be undervalued.

Venture capital   Involves an equity stake in a start-up or relatively young unlisted company.

Volume-weighted average price (VWAP)   The ratio of the value traded to total volume traded over a particular time horizon. It measures the average price a stock traded at over that time horizon. VWAP is often used in algorithmic trading and is used in the Market-Class 'dark pool' exchange in order to provide best execution price.

Wealth manager   Investment advisor professionals who specialise in financial planning, portfolio management and related financial services. They typically work with high net-worth individuals or small business owners.

Yield curve   A static function that relates the term to maturity to the yield to maturity for a sample of bonds at a given point in time. It therefore represents a cross-section of yields for a category of bonds that are comparable in all respects except their maturity.

Zero-coupon bond   A fixed-income interest that pays no coupon.

SOURCES AND WORKS CITED

Beniwal, Hermant. '15 Types of Risk That Affect Your Investments'. The Financial Literates RSS. N.p., n.d. Web. 19 Aug. 2013. www.tflguide.com/2011/09/types-of-risk.html.

Brown, Keith C. & Reilly, Frank K. (2009). *Investment Analysis and Portfolio Management*. 10th ed. USA: South-Western, Cengage Learning, p. 370.

'BondsOnline: Income Investor Tools'. BondsOnline. BondsOnline Group, Inc., n.d. Web. 18 Aug. 2013. www.bondsonline.com.

Central Fund of Canada home page. The Central Fund of Canada Limited, n.d. Web. 18 Aug. 2013. www.centralfund.com.

'Closed-End Funds'. Thomson Reuters, n.d. Web. 18 Aug. 2013. www.cefa.com.

'Derivative Financial Market'. SIX Swiss Exchange. SIX Swiss Exchange Ltd., n.d. Web. 19 Aug. 2013. www.six-swiss-exchange.com/knowhow/exchange/financial_market/derivative_market_en.html.

Dodd, Randall. 'What Are Money Markets?' *Finance & Development* (2012): 46. Print.

French, Kenneth R. 'The Cost of Active Investing'. March, 2008.

'Global Asset Management for Institutional Investors – Putnam Investments.' Putnam Investments. Putnam Retail Management, n.d. Web. 18 Aug. 2013. www.putnam.com/institutional.

Gu, Zhaoyang, and Jian, Xue. 'The Disciplining Role and Superiority of Independent Analysts'. Kellogg School of Management Research. Kellogg School of Management, Sept. 2006. Web. 18 Aug. 2013. www.stern.nyu.edu/sites/default/files/assets/documents/con_040525.pdf

'How Funds Work – Discounts and Charges.' Discounts and Charges. FIL Limited, n.d. Web. 18 Aug. 2013. www.fidelity.co.uk/investor/funds/funds-explained/discount-charges.page.

Ibbotson, Roger G., and Paul D. Kaplan. 2000. 'Does Asset Allocation Policy Explain 40, 90, or 100 Percent of Performance?' *Financial Analysts Journal*, vol. 56, no. 1 (January/February): 26–33.

Khorana, Ajay, and Servaes, Henri. 'On the Future of the Mutual Fund Industry Around the World'. *Pooling Money: The Future of Mutual Funds*, Brookings Institution (2008).

Khorana, Ajay, Servaes, Henri, and Tufano, Peter. 'Mutual fund fees around the world'. *Review of Financial Studies* 22, 3 (2009): 1279–1310.

'Lipper Leaders Ratings'. Leaders Ratings. Thomson Reuters, n.d. Web. 18 Aug. 2013. www.lipperweb.com/Research/Leaders.aspx.

Myners, Paul. 'Report on Institutional Investment.' HM Treasury, London (2001).

'OEICs'. OEIC Features. Lloyds Banking Group, n.d. Web. 18 Aug. 2013. www.scottishwidows.co.uk/investments/open_ended_investment_companies/in_detail.html.

'PIMCO Investment Basics'. *Everything You Need to Know about Bonds*. Pacific Investment Management Company, LLC, n.d. Web. 18 Aug. 2013. www.pimco.com/en/education/pages/everythingyouneedtoknowaboutbonds.aspx.

'Research on Hedge Funds, Fund of Funds, and Managed Futures / Alternative Investments'. Barclay Hedge. Barclay Hedge, LTD, n.d. Web. 18 Aug. 2013. www.barclayhedge.com.

Sharpe, William. 'The Sharpe Ratio'. *The Sharpe Ratio*. Stanford University, n.d. Web. 18 Aug. 2013. www.stanford.edu/~wfsharpe/art/sr/sr.htm.

'Smart401k®'. *Modern Portfolio Theory and The Efficient Frontier*. The Mutual Fund Research Center, n.d. Web. 19 Aug. 2013. www.smart401k.com/Content/retail/resource-center/advanced-investing/modern-portfolio-theory-and-the-efficient-frontier.

Sovereign Wealth Fund Institute, n.d. Web. 19 Aug. 2013. www.swfinstitute.org.

SPDR University. SPDRs Mobile. State Street Corporation, n.d. Web. 18 Aug. 2013. www.spdru.com.

'State Street Global Services'. Accounting Overview. State Street Corporation, n.d. Web. 18 Aug. 2013. www.statestreetglobalservices.com/wps/portal/internet/ssgs/home/capabilities/accounting/overview.

Taleb, Nassim Nicholas. *Fooled by Randomness: The Hidden Role of Chance in Life and in the Markets*. New York: Random House, 2005. Print.

Treasury Direct, n.d. Web. 19 Aug. 2013. www.treasurydirect.gov.

US Department of the Treasury, n.d. Web. 18 Aug. 2013. www.treasury.gov.

'Wealth Planning'. Wells Fargo Private Bank. Wells Fargo, n.d. Web. 18 Aug. 2013. www.wellsfargo.com/theprivatebank/oursolutions/wealthplanning.

'The World's Biggest Public Companies'. *Forbes* Magazine, n.d. Web. 19 Aug. 2013. www.forbes.com/global2000.

'Your Benefits I UBS Global Home'. UBS, n.d. Web. 18 Aug. 2013. www.ubs.com/global/en/wealth_management/your_goals-our_solutions/advisory_approach.html

Zhiguo He, Wei Xiong. 'Delegated Asset Management, Investment Mandates, and Capital Immobility'. *Journal of Financial Economics* 107.2 (2013):39+. Print

ACKNOWLEDGEMENTS

Writing a book that could complement our online simulation was always our dream. What better way to put yourself in the shoes of a professional portfolio manager than to read, learn and then put your new-found knowledge into practice?

It was that dream that gave us the time and energy to write the book, review it, edit, rewrite, edit, review it, and finally put the words into print. As most authors will probably testify, that energy and fuel comes from having a purpose and from the people around you – their inspiration and support.

Therefore, we would like to acknowledge the inspiration and support of the following in making our dream a reality. Our thanks go to Professor Ian Tonks at the University of Bath, whose initial enthusiasm and support in the creation of Market-Class was invaluable, and his subsequent recommendation that we produce a supporting book. To our business partner Edward Ivanovic, whose skills, abilities and tireless efforts brought our unique simulation and its 'exchange engine' to life. Our thanks go to Richard Willis and his team at Swales & Willis who helped us bring the first edition to market, and to Myles Hunt and Sally Tickner at Harriman House for their subsequent expertise and assistance in this latest edition. We thank Anna Stepanova for her incredible attention to detail and superior editing skills and Grace Myers Martin at Lexington Writing for her editing and advice on the writing style. To all our customers in the university and corporate sectors whose enthusiastic feedback about our unique simulation and the value it has brought their students, employees and customers alike provides perpetual enthusiasm to deliver more.

And finally, to our families who have supported us throughout our endeavours with Market-Class and whose support enables us to invest the many hours into our customers and resources like this book.

Thank you all.

Lightning Source UK Ltd.
Milton Keynes UK
UKOW07n0129290416

273209UK00002B/6/P

9 780857 194800